THE RUSSIAN REVOLUTION
1900–1927

12375

Studies in European History

General Editor: Richard Overy
Editorial Consultants: John Breuilly
                          Roy Porter

PUBLISHED TITLES

William Doyle, The Ancien Regime
R. W. Scribner, The German Reformation
Robert Service, The Russian Revolution 1900–1927

FORTHCOMING

T. W. Blanning, The French Revolution
Peter Burke, The Renaissance
Michael Dockrill, The Cold War 1945–1963
Geoffrey Ellis, The Napoleonic Empire
R. G. Geary, Labour Politics 1900–1930
Mark Greengrass, Calvinism in Early Modern Europe, *c.* 1560–1685
Henry Kamen, Golden Age Spain
Richard MacKenny, The City State and Urban Liberties, *c.* 1450–1650
Roger Price, The Revolutions of 1848
Geoffrey Scarre, Witchcraft and Magic in 16th and 17th Century Europe
Clive Trebilcock, Problems in European Industrialisation 1800–1914

THE RUSSIAN REVOLUTION 1900–1927

ROBERT SERVICE

M
MACMILLAN
EDUCATION

First published 1986
Reprinted 1987

Published by
MACMILLAN EDUCATION LTD
Houndmills, Basingstoke, Hampshire RG21 2XS
and London
Companies and representatives
throughout the world

Printed in Hong Kong

British Library Cataloguing in Publication Data
Service, Robert, 1947—
The Russian Revolution, 1900-1927.—(Studies
in European history)
1. Soviet Union—History—Nicholas II, 1894-1917
2. Soviet Union—History—1917-1936   3. Soviet
Union—Politics and government—1894-1917
4. Soviet Union—Politics and government—
1917-1936
I. Title   II. Series
947.08′3   DK246
ISBN 0-333-38819-4

List of Contents

vi

Editor's Preface

The main purpose of this new series of Macmillan studies is to make available to teacher and student alike developments in a field of history that has become increasingly specialised with the sheer volume of new research and literature now produced. These studies are designed to present the 'state of the debate' on important themes and episodes in European history since the sixteenth century, presented in a clear and critical way by someone who is closely concerned himself with the debate in question.

The studies are not intended to be read as extended bibliographical essays, though each will contain a detailed guide to further reading which will lead students and the general reader quickly to key publications. Each book carries its own interpretation and conclusions, while locating the discussion firmly in the centre of the current issues as historians see them. It is intended that the series will introduce students to historical approaches which are in some cases very new and which, in the normal course of things, would take many years to filter down into the textbooks and school histories. I hope it will demonstrate some of the excitement historians, like scientists, feel as they work away in the vanguard of their subject.

The format of the series conforms closely with that of the companion volumes of studies in economic and social history which has already established a major reputation since its inception in 1968. Both series have an important contribution to make in publicising what it is that historians are doing and in making history more open and accessible. It is vital for history to communicate if it is to survive.

R. J. OVERY

Introduction

The tossing of another stone onto the cairn of writings about
the Russian Revolution needs an explanation. Work on
modern Russia and the Soviet Union is on the increase. It has
enriched our knowledge of the country, but it is also leading to
compartmentalisation. Political, social and economic enquiries risk being closed off from each other. This book offers a
concise, integrated account. Many studies of the Revolution,
furthermore, resemble fragmented films of a long-jump. Some
deal with the run-up and take-off, ending the story in 1917;
others show the take-off and the jump, starting everything in
1917. And others, portraying only 1917, focus on the take-off.
There is room for an analysis with 1900 as the run's com-
mencement and 1927 as the landing point. The assessment of
continuities and disruptions is a prime objective. Another aim
is to strike a path away from traditional narrative treatments.
Key themes have been selected. They are signalled in each
chapter's subheadings. With so short a study, this makes
practical sense. It also lays the ground for comparing Russia's
transformation in the early twentieth century with what
happened elsewhere. The Revolution, of course, occurred
merely decades ago. A further intention is to show how
aspects of political and social life in today's USSR have their
origins in the Soviet historical experience.

Nothing in the following pages makes claim to originality;
and the brevity of the endnotes, in line with the scheme of the
series, necessarily obscures my debt to scholars whose works
are cited. Nor is the bibliography a list of all the fine
commentaries on the Revolution. It includes only books and
articles needed to corroborate specific points in the text.

Each chapter opens with a brief semi-caricature of older
accounts in order to throw basic issues into relief. Technical
vocabulary has been minimised. Dates are given according to

the contemporary official calendar. A simplified version of the SEER transliteration code is used, but well-known names like Witte retain their usual English form. Quantitative data are controversial; an attempt has been made to supply figures not subject to fundamental dispute. As regards terminology, I have kept to the old Russian definition of large factories as being those employing at least sixteen workers with some motor-power or at least thirty without. John Channon, Julian Cooper, Bob Davies, Arfon Rees, Mike Smith, Steve Wheatcroft and Howard White gave permission to cite their unpublished studies. The book's drafts underwent much revision. For their reading of the chapters I am grateful to Roger Bartlett, Adele Biagi, Olga Crisp, Bob Davies, Graeme Gill, Alan Hall, Jill Hall, Geoffrey Hosking, Evan Mawdsley, Richard Overy, Arfon Rees and Steve Wheatcroft. Their criticisms invariably made for improvements. In addition, Steve Wheatcroft's replies to supplementary questions on agriculture in 1917–21 gave invaluable assistance; and I have gained great benefit, since moving to London, from discussions with Olga Crisp about the pre-war Russian economy.

Emma Service typed in the final corrections, and Owain, Hugo and Francesca gave other practical help. I am grateful to all four of them.

London
September 1985

Israel Getzler has kindly suggested several amendments for this second printing.

A Note on References

References are cited throughout in brackets according to the numbering in the bibliography, with page references where necessary indicated by a colon after the bibliography number.

1 · The Unstable Compound, 1900–1914

Visitors to the Russian empire before the First World War returned with similar accounts. Critics and admirers reported that the regime in St Petersburg had an undiminished capacity for oppression. Russian society, in their estimation, was changeless. Peasantry and workers were 'dark masses'. The universal level of their living conditions, low for centuries, had recently been forced down further by heavy direct taxation. 'Modernisation' remained slight. The Russian imperial state was uniformly reactionary. It acted exclusively in its own interests and was unresponsive to pressure by any social class. And western socialists and liberals (and even many conservatives) had no doubt that such a situation was the chief cause for the recurrence of revolutionary crisis in Russia. This summary, whether wholly or in its various parts, continued to attract widespread favour after 1917 and retains many supporters even today.

(i) St Petersburg and the world in 1900

Those contemporary observers took it as axiomatic that the removal of Nikolai II's absolute powers would have largely solved all political, social and economic problems. Yet the country confronted difficulties around the turn of the century which were not surmountable simply by a change of regime. Looked at from St Petersburg, the world outside the Russian borders had never seemed more threatening. Peace in Europe was brittle. Two great powers, France and Prussia, had gone to war against each other in 1870. The unification of Germany gave her dominance in the politics and trade of the continent's

1

central regions; and her ally, Austria-Hungary, strove to exert greater influence in the Balkans. The quest for security led Russia to sign an alliance with France in 1894. But the German government also posed a challenge in Persia and the Near East. Crises in diplomatic relations recurred. In addition, Japan effected rapid industrialisation and became a major power in the Far East. The era was the apogee of imperialist aggrandisement. China was the largest prey, and Russia extracted consent that northern China lay within its sphere of control. Russian imperialism had a long history. Ukrainian, Siberian, Baltic, Polish and Transcaucasian lands had been conquered. As recently as the 1870s, the army had been sent to subjugate areas in central Asia; and with the Ottoman empire on the brink of dissolution, Petersburg's diplomats hoped for the acquisition of the Straits of the Dardanelles.

Complacency was not in order. Any government in Russia wishing to prevent domination by foreign states or even territorial dismemberment had to stimulate what is nowadays known as 'modernisation'. Britain, France, Germany and the USA had effected it. The use of steam power and, latterly, electricity in factories transformed their economies. Their armed forces acquired a massive technical advantage, and their educational facilities had been expanded to provide training in the mental skills newly necessary in every walk of life. Accepting the task 'late' in the day, the Russian regime was under the more urgent pressure to accomplish it. This was no unusual problem. Countries like Italy and Spain confronted it, and others in Africa, Asia and South America do to this day.

Yet Russia had other predicaments which made her unique among the rival powers of Europe. The climate was extremely unhelpful. Vast tracts of Siberia lie above permafrost, and parts of central Asia are desert. Russia proper has more clement weather. But winter in Moscow is much longer than in London, Paris and New York. Soil quality leaves a lot to be desired. Only limited areas, principally in the southern Ukraine and the southern steppes, approach the fertility of North America's cereal-growing belts. The Russian empire's size, too, was no unqualified asset. It is fully 5000 miles from eastern Poland, which was then administered directly from St Petersburg, to Vladivostok on the Pacific coast; and 2000 miles lie between Murmansk in the frozen north and the Turkish frontier. The domain of the Russian emperor dwarfed the land mass of any other state. The USA and Brazil were small by comparison. The impediments to transport were immense: it was an unfortunate accident of geography that the main navigable rivers flowed away from economic centres. The dispersal of raw materials was an additional drawback. Gold and timber came from Siberia, oil from Baku by the Caspian. Petersburg became the main site for the metal-processing industries, but coal and iron were in their abundance hundreds of miles away in the Donets Basin. Ethnic diversity complicated the problem. Russians constituted only two fifths of their land-based empire's population. Poles, Latvians, Ukrainians and Azeris had regional majorities in places vital to the country's industrial health.

Russia's modernisation could hardly fail to be especially arduous. Economic backwardness encouraged the quest for transformation at a faster tempo than in rival countries, and this was bound to unsettle a social order already in perilous flux. And both climate and topography entailed financial costs higher than elsewhere.

(ii) The absolute monarchy before 1905

Strong state power would be required to prevail upon the labour force to forgo drastic immediate raising of its living standards; firm direction would also be necessary to co-ordinate the economy's advance. The Russian state was headed by an absolute monarchy. The Romanov dynasty had ruled since 1613, and no emperor in the nineteenth century had shared power with an elective, representative assembly. Parties were banned. Public meetings were strictly controlled, and a pre-publication press censorship was applied. Rebellion was rare. Regicide occurred in 1762 and 1801. But these were coups which replaced one royal incumbent with another. Even the unsuccessful popular revolt raised in 1773 by

3

Emelyan Pugachev against Catherine II lacked the aim of basic reform. Not until 1825 was a truly revolutionary organisation formed. It took shape as a conspiracy of army officers and other nobles; and it, too, was easily crushed. Nikolai I, who was crowned in 1826, retained massive authority for himself and his successor Aleksandr II. A personal cult of the emperor was encouraged. It was largely effective. Peasants cherished an icon of the ruler on their hut walls. And the emperor's word was law, quite literally. A simple, oral instruction could overrule any previous legislation. Regal 'arbitrariness' was therefore systematic. The Council of Ministers in the last century, furthermore, bore little resemblance to a British cabinet: it held no collective deliberations. Every minister was kept responsible to the monarch alone (142:*21–2*). It was also the crown which appointed the governors who directed the organs of provincial government. Such bureaucrats were invested with huge powers; and the police in the localities had the right to mete out punishments by administrative fiat.

Whether this structure could adequately grapple with the tasks facing the Russian state at the end of the nineteenth century is doubtful. But unqualified dismissal would be anachronistic. It was still in the not so distant past, in 1789, that France's absolute monarchy had been dismantled. In addition, parliamentary democracy was cramped even in the United Kingdom; the British franchise was extended to all male adults only in 1884. Repression of anti-establishment groups persisted longer elsewhere. The German social-democrats remained outlawed until 1890. In the USA, some employers got away with violent harassment of socialists well into the 1930s. The Russian monarchy was an extreme case of authoritarianism in a world which knew many gradations of unfreedom.

Nevertheless the rulers became aware of the need for economic transformation. Aleksandr III, mounting the throne in 1881, was a consistent industrialiser. Nikolai II acceded in 1894. Neither was intellectually inspired or inspiring, and the emperor Nikolai was an incorrigible vacillator. But their support for industrial growth was solid. Sergei Witte, Minister of Finance from 1892 to 1903, noted the uses of autocracy, and with some reason. A Russian parliament elected through a universal adult franchise would have turned the peasantry's demographic predominance into political dominion. The peasant would have become the maker of governments. His preferences would have included a lowering of taxation and, in financial policy, a higher priority for the sector producing agricultural goods. Crucial state investment would have declined. Several heavy industries, especially in the field of armaments, would have suffered badly. Perhaps the same difficulties would not have arisen should the autocracy have granted a franchise limited to the propertied classes. This had been the pattern of German modernisation (and the Japanese employed it successfully in the 1890s). But industrialists were proportionately fewer in Russia, and the Russian landed nobility contained a larger body of opinion hostile to industrial enterprise. Emulation of Germany would have created its own problems. Be that as it may, a resolute autocrat in St Petersburg could play a helpful role in stimulating and defending industrialisation. Aleksandr III and Nikolai II did so. The bourgeoisie made progress under their protection.

Every state has internal divisions. The Ministry of Internal Affairs, aware of the risks of pushing the peasantry too hard, warned against fast industrial expansion (100:*417–18*). Other institutions were less obstructive. The Orthodox church acted loyally as the government's power spiritual. But the incomprehension of priests was legendary, and their assistance to the drive for economic modernisation was negligible. Thousands of officials in the civil bureaucracy also were apathetic or simply bemused. Venality was widespread. Nepotism and incompetence were a national shame. Furthermore, ministerial competition for resources was intense. The standing army was a drain on the exchequer; its duty to complete the subjugation of the Caucasus and hold down eastern Poland was costly. But the Ministry of Finance acquitted itself well in the struggle over the budget. The regime as a whole was in the grip of transition. The state administration was not just a form of exclusive indoor relief for nobles who had failed at farming. In reality, four-fifths of posts in the highest four grades of the civil service before the First World War were held by men who were not landed gentry; and non-nobles had become a majority in the army officer corps by 1912 (70:*401*).

5

(iii) Economic progress

And the government's handling of industry was impressive. State ownership and state contracts contributed vitally to capitalist economic development in Russia. The possession of weapon-producing factories had been a traditional objective of the authorities; but the railways too were recognised for their importance: two-thirds of the network in 1914 were state property. Increasing revenues were obviously necessary. The myth persists that industrialisation was achieved through a universal immiseration of the peasantry. Yet the largest portion of the government's income, 40 per cent in 1913, came from customs and excise duties (17:*4*). *Central* direct taxes were comparatively low; even Witte, hardly the peasant's friend, treated an expansion of rural purchasing capacity (albeit rigorously contained within limits) as indispensable. The government in any event could not finance development solely from its own coffers. Less than a ninth of the industrial capital stock was in its hands at the outbreak of the First World War (14:*51–2*). Domestic private enterprise was nurtured. The 'monster tariff' of 1891 gave protection; it also induced foreign companies to set up branches inside the Russian empire whereas before they had exported. The decision of 1897 to put the rouble on the gold standard attracted further investment from abroad. It is estimated that foreigners owned 47 per cent of Russian securities, excluding mortgage bonds, by 1914 (14:*154*).

There were dangers in relying so heavily upon injections of capital from western Europe. These were recognised by Witte. But he astutely predicted that a massive withdrawal of funds would not occur. Russian creditworthiness was excellent, and profits were solid. French and Belgian finance led the way in boosting activity on the St Petersburg stock exchange. At any rate, Russian industrial development was not deflected by foreign interest groups from a course that would otherwise have been adopted by successive emperors. Russia was not Bulgaria. Its government was not so easily intimidated (119:*531–3*).

The world trade cycle, however, was beyond its control, and the Russian economy remained vulnerable to the periodic

6

recessions in the rest of Europe. The slump between 1900 and 1903 was damaging. Yet the country also benefited from Europe's booms, and by 1914 the empire was the fifth largest industrial power on earth. The growth rates were imposing. Industrial output expanded annually by 8 per cent in the 1890s and by 6 per cent between 1907 and the beginning of the Great War (37:*149*). The railways were expanded in the 1860s. 30,000 miles of track were laid in the pre-war period. Russia became the world's fourth greatest producer of coal, pig-iron and steel. Oil extraction, too, was successful. The Baku fields were seriously rivalled only by Texas. But areas of weakness remained. The chemical, electrical and machine-tool industries gave cause for concern (30:*12*). Even so, factories in Russia were starting to turn out lathes, locomotives and motor cars. Capital goods were prominent in the country's economic progress. But they were not the only sphere of endeavour. Mass consumer demands increased. Textiles continued to be Russia's biggest single industry through to the First World War; and together with food-processing they supplied 50 per cent of total industrial output value (whereas the figure was 14 per cent for mining and metallurgy) (14:*34–5*) The balance between capital and consumer products was not particularly unusual for a country at Russia's stage of modernisation (44:*430*).

Thus the economy was not all guns and no butter. The suggestion that industrial advance was achieved by agricultural regression is unproved. Russian agrarian indices point to a moderate advance. The harvests of wheat and other cereals, which were the mainstay of national agriculture, increased in the second half of the nineteeth century (84: *284*) A famine afflicted the Volga region in 1891–2. Climate could play havoc with even the best-organised farms (136: *27–8*) And yet improvement, despite intermittent set-backs, was solid. Grain output rose by an annual average of 2 per cent between 1881 and 1913 in European Russian (or by 1.1 million tons per annum) (135:*3*).

This achievement was passed over in silence by the regime's disparagers. The imperial population increased steeply in the second half of the nineteenth century, so that much of the benefit of the agricultural expansion was lost. Yet per capita cereal production in European Russia still rose, possibly by as much as 35 per cent from 1890 to 1913 (52:*270*). Russia became the largest cereal exporter in the world. In the half-decade before the First World War it sold abroad an annual average of 11.5 million tons (135: *2*). Its agriculture was also beginning to diversify. Potatoes and dairy products gained in commercial significance, especially in Poland and the Baltic region. It was the Ukraine and southern Russia, with the Urals and western Siberia, that were responsible for the expansion in wheat output. Sugar-beet emerged as an important crop; the area given over to it, mainly in the Ukraine, rose by 38 per cent in the decade before the Great War (23:*225*). Nor were industrial crops ignored. Cotton-growing was penetrating Turkestan's economy. The prospect of further progress in the empire's agriculture as a whole grew strong. Sales of machines and other equipment increased. Investment in such stock appears to have risen at an annual rate of 9 per cent from 1891 to 1913 (45: *274*).

(iv) The transforming of Russian society

It is irrefutable, on the other hand, that the modernisation of both industry and agriculture still had a long, long way to go. Few cities were yet miniature versions of St Petersburg, and villages by the thousand slumbered on unacquainted with novel techniques of production. Change was geographically patchy. It was also prone to the menace of ever fiercer foreign competitiveness. Furthermore, the Russian government's contribution was not exclusively helpful. Its financial policies and its orders for railways and armaments aided industrial growth. It was less solicitous about agriculture. Peasants in particular felt that they were left to fend for themselves, and that the land bank established for them in 1882 merely scratched the surface of their problems. And not even the government's defenders claimed that its encouragement of industry was comprehensive. In any case, ministerial bureaucracies were not the sole agents of modernisation. Social forces supplied massive momentum. Indeed the spurt of officially-fostered industrialisation in the 1880s and 1890s was preceded by decades when state policies had been inimical in some ways to industrialism as such.

An example of this was the regime's endeavour in the nineteenth century to preserve the peasant land commune. Regulations compelled a rural lad to seek permission from the village elders to leave for work in the towns; such a stipulation reflected the government's wish to curtail the enlargement of the landless poor. It used to be thought that the desire was fulfilled. After all, there were only 3.1 million workers in factories and mines in 1913. But the working class included other groups too. The addition of railwaymen, builders, waiters, home-based workers and domestic servants yields a total of 15 million (20 million if agricultural wage-labourers are taken into account) (97:*329,333*). This was a fourfold increase over 1860. Growing industries required a growth in the provision of basic schooling. The government, too, wished to expand educational and social amenities if only to emulate competing powers in Europe. From 1864 it allowed the election of organs of rural self-government, known as *zemstva*, with limited responsibilities for schools, roads and hospitals; and the existing municipal councils were strengthened so as to fulfil similar local tasks. Central government itself put a vast school-building programme in hand. Nearly two-thirds of all factory workers in European Russia, according to a survey in 1918, were literate; and, in metropolitan printing and metal-processing plants, reading and writing accomplishments were well-nigh universal (97:*601*).The Russian worker's similarity to his counterpart in Germany or Britain should not be overstated. Most members of the industrial workforce kept in touch with their native villages. Retention of plots of land was commonplace (66:*139*). But the movement towards the formation of a 'hereditary working class', schooled to read books and trained to operate complex machinery, was firmly under way.

The villages left behind by these workers changed less than the towns, but were not unchanging. An Emancipation Edict was issued in 1861. It was the start of the series of reforms in the same decade. Until then the peasantry, which constituted nine-tenths of the population, was legally tied in personal bondage to the owners of the land where they were born or

9

consisted of state peasants under the tutelage of governmental officials. The nobility and the royal family were the country's greatest private landowners. But their peasants, while being made free as persons, received an unfavourable economic settlement. The average amount of land obtained by them across the empire, excluding Poland, was 13 per cent less than they had previously cultivated; and in the more fertile regions, such as in southern Russia, the nobility made the peasants forgo as much as a third or even a half of what they had previously tilled (36:*730*).

Matters, however, did not stand still at that. The physical terrain held as property by nobles proceeded to diminish. Sell-ups became a stampede after 1905. It is reckoned that the nobility had owned twice as much land in the 1860s as it retained by 1912 (2:*87*). Absentee landlordism was also on the increase. Many estates were rented out. Townspeople were among those who took over the noble estates, but the majority of the new owners and tenants were former serfs. The peasantry's share in the agricultural economy, far from being compressed, expanded remarkably. Buying and renting of land occurred so massively that close to nine-tenths of European Russia's sown area by 1916 was under cultivation by peasants (64:*182*). Four-fifths of the agricultural machines in use in 1910 belonged to them (22:*264*), and possibly as much as 87 per cent of the total value of the empire's agricultural output between 1909 and 1913 was produced by them (64:*190*). The expansion of a market economy shook age-old village customs. So, too, did the spread of literacy. Progress was understandably slower than in the towns; but surveys of a dozen provinces in European Russia before the Great War revealed that about two-fifths of the male rural population had learnt at least to read and write their own names (98:*294*). Evidently life in the countryside was not yet utterly transformed; but the achievement was not trivial, and the drive towards new styles of existence had begun in earnest.

In addition, not all nobles went bankrupt. Many who left the land departed only because they were offered outrageously good prices or because jobs in the civil service or even business beckoned (63:*124–6*). Owners of large farms in the southern Ukraine and in the Baltic region, furthermore, showed little

10

sign of giving way to their peasant rivals as producers (1:*382–4*; 81:*29*). These became successful capitalists. The gentry marketed twice as large a proportion of its harvest as the peasants did of theirs (64:*188*). The incentive for such a social group to seek political reform was small. Noble land-owners were not without resentment of the industrial bourgeoisie; and in 1898 they secured a modification of the tariff system which protected the growth of factories in Russia. Dues payable on imports of agricultural machinery were scrapped. There was also a successful campaign, guided by the Minister of Internal Affairs V. K. Pleve, to lobby the emperor against a proposal to confer noble status upon distinguished non-noble figures in trade and industry (63:*151–2*; 118:*301–3*). Yet such industrialists and bankers could count their blessings. The state, with its contracts and its help in cases of trouble with the workforce, was too valuable for the urban capitalist to strain after its overthrow. And, as for the rural capitalist, his grievances had more huff and puff than real bite: the Ministry of Finance so arranged the railway freight rates as to make it especially cheap for him to find his markets inside and outside the country (56:*173–4*).

(v) Social discontents

Especially dangerous elements of discontent did not yet exist widely among the propertied classes in the same density as at lower levels of the social order. With the development of the working class in the towns there came a multitude of problems. Russian factory workers were poor: many were earning only enough for subsistence. They were subjected to harsh and humiliating treatment at work. Safety regulations were widely ignored. Foremen could fine labourers for minor or even imaginary infringements of rules. The average working day, without overtime, was between twelve and fourteen hours in the 1880s (59:*42,47*). Housing was bad: for the majority the choice lay between spartan company 'barracks' and costly, unhygienic, overcrowded rented rooms. These conditions do a lot to explain the rebelliousness which was to make the Russian working class legendary in 1905 and 1917.

11

Such squalor was not unique to Russia. While sections of the industrial workforce in countries like Britain and Germany were beginning to enjoy a somewhat more comfortable life by the turn of the century, even western Europe contained areas of dreadful misery. Workers in Milan, for example, were typically little better off than those in St Petersburg – and, not surprisingly, the spirit of revolt flourished in both cities. Of course, not all Russian labourers were rebels. The accusation used to be made that the trouble came mostly from the unskilled 'raw youths' from the countryside who swarmed into the towns and occasionally formed unruly mobs. But this fails to account for the quiescence of Irish immigrants to Birmingham. Furthermore, it is evident from analyses of industrial conflicts in Russia that the leadership and inspiration came from the more skilled and more urbanised sections of the workforce (8:*210*). As elsewhere in Europe, such workers tended to have the understanding and the organisational capacity to take up the struggle. A slight rise in average real wages occurred between 1900 and 1913 (13:*407*). But it was the slightness of the improvement and not the improvement itself that was impressive to most workers.

Poor conditions and rising expectations produced turbulence in Britain, France and Germany in this period. Strikes in Russia were not spectacularly large or frequent before the turn of the century; 1899 was the peak year of the decade for industrial conflict, and yet the number of the strikers was only 97,000 (62:*225*). But the maintained ban on trade unions aggravated tension. This was recognised in all major industrial countries, albeit only eventually and often with reservations, except Russia. The sheer rapidity of industrialisation made channels for the expression of grievances vital; and the gigantic size of many factories in Russia exacerbated the sense of the gulf between employers and employed. Two-fifths of workers in plants and works belonged to workforces of over 1000 in 1914 (57:*7*).

The peasants, apart from some disturbances in the early 1860s and late 1870s, did not put the police to much bother in the last century. Yet their unhappiness was intense. It infuriated them that so much of the territory they cultivated, especially before 1905, had to be rented from gentry landown-

12

ers (who were also hated for retaining crucial pastures and woods). This detracted large advantage from the peasantry's rise in income. In any case, the rise was an aggregate figure which disguised the gradations of living standards. Most peasants lived in communes. And this institution was used by the government as a cost-free, tax-gathering facility. Communes in central and northern Russia, furthermore, periodically redistributed their land among resident peasant households. But material inequalities survived, and the more affluent peasants, known as kulaks, frequently hired the others in the village as labourers or else became the local money-lenders. The Russian village poor were miserably poor, by most European if not the Indian standards of the day. Even few kulaks were in the same league as middling smallholders in Bavaria or France. This concentrated minds powerfully on the land question. Peasant land-hunger was near-universal, and the belief that noble landowners should be constrained to give up their land was deeply held. Then there were all the discriminatory laws. Peasants, until 1904, were subject to corporal punishment for misdemeanours; and the institution of 'land captains', who were charged with keeping order in the villages and who often were from the gentry, was a further vexation.

(vi) Political upheaval: 1905–6

The possibility that the discontent might turn into political opposition was the government's nightmare in the late nineteenth century. Enlightened labour laws were passed. But implementation was patchy, and the army was used to break up strikes. This meant that conflicts over wages between employers and employees automatically acquired a political significance. Workers increasingly discerned this. So too did students. Their governmentally-appointed deans, their mandatory uniforms and their niggardly grants annoyed them. Postgraduate unemployment was a further factor (91:45–6). It is true that the bureaucracy gave jobs to numerous ex-students, and that state enterprises like the railways were major employers. But a ponderous insistence upon hierarchy and routine continued to be confronted by a frustrated young generation through to the end of the regime. Some therefore entrenched themselves in the 'free professions' like law and medicine. Others made their mark in the zemstva (29:*426–8*).

For members of this intelligentsia it was an unchallengeable premise that the absolute monarchy was the primordial cause of the country's ills. Clandestine organisations were formed from the 1860s onwards. They aimed to refound society on the basis of the traces of egalitarianism in the peasant land commune. Their focusing upon 'the people' earned them their description as 'populists' (or *narodniki*), and they argued that a transition directly to a socialist order was practicable. A party, Land And Freedom, operated in the 1870s. It recruited hundreds of peasants. But the vast rural majority never knew its name. Its propaganda had little effect; and the assassination of the emperor Aleksandr II by its terrorist off-shoot, People's Freedom, caused national revulsion in 1881. Yet an estimated 5000 revolutionaries resumed activity in the political 'underground' in the ensuing two decades (82:*42*). The populists came to recognise that capitalism was planting deep roots in the Russian economy, and that the urban working class was more responsive than the bafflingly quiescent peasantry to political slogans. Secret unions were formed, at great risk, by the workers themselves from 1874 onwards. Political liberty was among their demands. Populists strove to enter and direct such organisations. From the 1880s they were rivalled by groupings which adapted the doctrines of German social-democracy to conditions in Russia. These new Russian Marxists hymned large-scale social units and urbanism; in their view, a bourgeois-led republican government had to be placed in power before there could be talk of a further transition to socialism. Their outlook won more supporters than populism in the late 1890s. But the link-up with the mass labour movement was realised only fitfully. Police rounded up activists in their hundreds. Liberals were harassed; the neo-populists, the Socialist-Revolutionaries, suffered prison and exile. And the Russian Marxists, whose 10,000 adherents made them the largest anti-monarchist party in 1904, were hunted hard (112:*25*).

Yet repression did not work well enough for the government. Other preventive measures were tried. The sundry

14

pieces of legislation discriminating against the peasantry
began to be repealed after the turn of the century. Attention
was directed at the workers too. A few trade unions were
legalised, but with harsh restrictions and under strict police
surveillance. Quickly the experiment was adjudged dangerous
by the Ministry of the Interior and was under threat by 1904
(108:*189–90*).

It was the remnants of one such union in St Petersburg, led
by an Orthodox Church priest, Georgi Gapon, that induced
upheaval in the following year. Rostov-on-Don had been in
tumult in 1902; street demonstrations had been pacified by
troops. Petersburg in 1905 was less easily controlled. On 9
January, guards units fired upon Gapon's peaceful procession
in favour of constitutional and social reforms. 'Bloody Sunday' provoked strikes and public marches. The non-Russian
nationalities grasped their opportunity. The Poles, especially
in Warsaw and Lodz, defied the government. Finland and
Georgia fell into commotion. The armed forces, moreover,
were engaged in war with Japan from 1904, and their defeats
increased the regime's unpopularity. Rebellion at home intensified. Workers in every city created their own sectional,
elective councils. The Russian word for council is *soviet*. These
councils, evolving beyond the functions of strike leadership,
set up administrative apparatuses. Political revolution loomed
nearer. Peasants, their harvest ruined by drought, were
restive. Illegal pasturing and woodfelling on gentry land
occurred in the summer, and agricultural wage-labourers
struck for more pay. Cases of arson increased. Occasional
seizures of land occurred. Village communes, wherever they
existed, helped to co-ordinate the anti-gentry revolt. A
Peasants' Union was established nationally. But the rebels in
the countryside acted independently; it was in the towns that
large organisations made an impact. Men, not surprisingly in
view of the Russian family's structure, took a bigger part than
women (43:*81–2*). Trade unions were formed even among
civil servants, waiters and the unemployed. Factory workers
were not alone on the streets. Industrialists had begun to
doubt the government's technical competence; they too, at
least initially, joined the clamour for a constitution. The
political parties emerged from clandestinity. Mutiny erupted
in the Black Sea fleet. The Marxist leadership of the Moscow

15

Soviet mounted an armed uprising of workers in December 1905.

(vii) The limits of the regime's adaptiveness

Two principal factors saved the regime: its unsparing use of the army (and the hangings and beatings of villagers led to protests world-wide); and the last-ditch promise of political concessions in the October Manifesto of 1905. Opposition was either quelled or deflected. A parliament, or *Duma*, was promised. It duly met in April 1906. Its powers were narrowly limited. It could not appoint ministers, it could not hold the government responsible to it. It could not pass laws autonomously. It was also liable to dissolution at the emperor's behest. And yet a chastened Nikolai II was nonetheless willing to display favour toward leaders of Russian liberalism. He invited a few, including Pavel Milyukov, into the Council of Ministers. This kind of political semi-compromise was not a Russian invention. It existed in Germany through to 1918. But the offer came too late in Russia and its empire. It would have been a difficult trick to pull off earlier in any case; but the liberals, who called themselves the Constitutional Democrats (or Kadets), spurned the proposal. They held out for the granting of a parliament with independent legislative authority. Liberals in the First Duma harangued ministers. But the Duma, to their horror, was disbanded by imperial decree. The monarch and his premier P. A. Stolypin were no more enamoured of the Second Duma; and in 1907, with something of a coup d'état, they altered the electoral rules so that the landed gentry might dominate the new chamber. The Third State Duma was the result. Its largest party were conservatives known as the Octobrists; they accepted the limits of political behaviour newly imposed, and aimed to gain an influence over the government by co-operating with it in the Duma.

Stolypin, not wanting to rely too heavily upon the nobility in the countryside, tried to strengthen the peasantry's rights in the local elections to the zemstva (50:*155*). His attempt was frustrated. It ran athwart the nobility's interests, and Nikolai

II acceded to requests to maintain the status quo. Gentry landowners set their face against sharing their rural dominance even with neighbouring industrialists (75:*369–70*). In any case, Stolypin's own ambitions had their contradictions. He arranged that the peasantry's demographic strength was not duly registered in the Third Duma; he also wanted the peasant 'ringleaders' of 1905 hanged. Field courts-martial summarily sent 2694 such men and women to their death by 1909 (26:*448*).

Stolypin himself was killed by an assassin in 1911; but his political fortunes had long been in eclipse. The emperor was his own empire's greatest landowner. He remained reluctant to go against the wishes of the landowning class. He had never been keen about constitutional reform, and steadily the will to preserve his dynasty's powers intact supervened over all other desires. In 1909 he took offence at Stolypin's proposal that, in order to keep sound relations with the Octobrists, the Duma should be permitted to vet matters like the imperial navy's budget. He sought out congenial advisers. The court was attended by mystics, quacks and the reputed 'holy man' Rasputin. Ministerial office became more and more closely associated with bribery and corruption. Honest crown servants like Witte and Stolypin gave way to toadies. There were those at court who made criticisms. But they castigated the symptoms of decadence, not the disease: they reviled Rasputin and yet eschewed contemplation of basic political problems. The quasi-constitutional settlement of 1906 involved an Imperial State Council as a counter-weight to the far from weighty Duma. The State Council was drawn from the higher spheres of state, church, zemstva, business and landed nobility; its very conservative majority regularly upset initiatives for change emanating from the Duma and from Stolypin (26:*491*). This suited the emperor's purposes. His nominations to the State Council reflected his rigidity. Such a milieu of people and institutions would doubtless have been a considerable impediment even if he had determined upon a course of political innovation.

Nationalism became the regime's last stand-by. Covert support was given to organisations such as the Black Hundreds which fomented massacres of Jews in the west of the empire and plundered their homes and possessions. Traditional chauvinism also took non-violent forms. The Orthodox Church, constrained to act as the ecclesiastical arm of government, confined its creativity mainly to increasing intolerance towards the other Christian denominations and the Moslems. The Ministry of Foreign Affairs loudly asserted Russia's status as protector of the Slavs in the Balkans.

(viii) Social resilience and institutional growth

Yet the monarchy's power was on the wane. It is true that the revolutionaries had been spectacularly crushed: the organised adherents of Marxism fell in number from 150,000 in 1907 to 10,000 in 1910 (28:*36–7*). But the government's suppressive capacity was much greater in brief, intense trials of strength than in the perennial political struggle. The police state was still only half-built. Indeed the Russian empire had seven times fewer policemen as a ratio of the total population than the United Kingdom (105:*56*). This comparison can mislead. No account is taken of the garrison troops used to keep the peace, nor of village 'self-policing'. Even so, the control of civil society became more problematic after 1905 when the limitations on state power had been exposed. It was hard enough to keep tabs on oppositional activities. It was harder still to regulate the spread of ideas, and the censorship's grip was importantly relaxed in 1906 when a law was passed relieving publishers of the requirement to submit manuscripts before publication. Successive censors had been inefficient. *Das Kapital* had appeared legally in 1872. The roll of honour of Russian literature includes authors, from Aleksandr Pushkin through to Lev Tolstoi and Maksim Gorki, who evaded the banning of their works by dressing up their objections to the political system in indirect but yet accessible language. The terminology became less restrained before the First World War. Printing presses were still often fined and occasionally closed down by the authorities, but even the revolutionary parties managed to resume publication. Usually they simply renamed their newspapers and continued printing as previously.

The size of the country and the slowness of communications ruled out any more effective clamp-down. A chronological perspective is also needed. Not all the technological innovations that facilitated the extremely repressive states headed by Stalin in the Soviet Union and Hitler in Germany had yet been disseminated. In addition, the government did not regard such excesses of regimentation as an objective. The executions of 1906–9 were more the exception than the norm. Exile was the usual punishment for political dissenters (although many, being too poor to afford the rail fare, had to travel to Siberia on foot and died *en route*) (140:*23*).

On the other hand, the regime's efforts to mobilise popular favour behind it were diminutive. They could even be counter-productive. The coronation of Nikolai II in 1895 was planned so ham-fistedly that hundreds of onlookers on Khodynka field were trampled to death. Later state occasions, such as the celebration of the Romanov dynasty's tercentenary in 1913, were better arranged; but governing circles in St Petersburg lacked the imaginativeness of their counterparts in Berlin or London in developing new rituals to establish cohesion between state and society. The Russian emperor, of course, ruled a congeries of mutually hostile nationalities, and Russians constituted only 45 per cent of his subjects. It was very difficult to obtain the approval of Poles and Finns without allowing them to secede. The Ukrainians and Belorussians, who were ethnically closer to the Russians, were not so implacable, and, in the Transcaucasus, the Armenians were particularly aware that independence would expose them to the threat of a Turkish invasion (113:*665–70*). But the authorities did little to enhance their reputation among non-Russians. And chances to rally backing from Russians, too, were overlooked – except for the dreadful anti-semitism of officials. This neglectfulness was not confined to the government. The middle classes in Russia seldom founded the football clubs, choral societies and building projects which fostered civic pride and, to some extent, an inter-class culture in the West (104:*36,39*). Probably social antagonisms were anyway too unyielding. Cultural integration can succeed only if based on symbols of unity which induce a sympathetic resonance in society. All the same, there were few campaigns of even a philanthropic nature. The zemstva ran some hospitals, but the resultant tax burden was resented by peasants, and in the towns, a few 'people's houses' were privately established to supply workers with reading clubs (51:*77–8*).

Consequently workingmen, being culturally insulated from the state and the middle classes, organised their own groupings. From the mid-nineteenth century they were forming Sunday schools. These were devoted to initiating or broadening the education of the adult pupils, and they attracted revolutionaries as volunteer teachers. Another point of activity were the sick-funds (even though they had by law to include employers' representatives). Taverns were a favourite gathering spot. The growth of atheism and alcoholism caused official anxiety; but labourers befuddled by vodka were not a threat to the regime. Other modes of social intercourse were, especially the groups of workers linked by common geographical origins and known as *zemlyachestva*. In these, a man could relax and talk without fear of the police (51:*77–8*). The legalisation of trade unions in October 1905, furthermore, led to a proliferation of still larger organisations. Admittedly about 600 unions were shut down by 1911. But some always survived, and their adminstrations trained hundreds of working-class functionaries to handle office business. The co-operative movement, too, flourished. Thousands of agricultural co-ops existed by 1914 (53:*14*). They also encountered bureaucratic harassment, but this only increased the alienation of their largely peasant membership from the political status quo. Independent social organisations, despite interference, were a fact of life. 'Autocratic Russia' was no longer run completely autocratically.

(ix) Economic problems before 1914

Even before 1905 the government had seen agrarian reform as its main hope of survival. The rural turbulence in that year convinced opinion in official and landowning circles that the peasant commune, far from acting as a prop for the existing order of things, undermined the foundations. Communal agriculture was associated with three-field crop rotation; with

20

the division of each field into several strips for each household; and, in European Russia, with periodic redistributions of land among households. Russian peasant agriculture, for all its advances, remained backward by the standards of the western great powers. Stolypin's initial wish, when he became premier in 1906, was for the peasants to disband the commune, consolidate a household's strips of land into a contiguous holding, and hand property deeds to the existing heads of household. Independent, prosperous smallholders were his goal.

In fact, only about a tenth of peasant households in the empire's European zone consolidated by 1916 (24:*572, 583*). The government had made the terms of exodus from the commune increasingly easy. Even so, the fall of individual applications to leave after 1909 was never reversed. The reform's warmest welcome occurred in the fertile south of the empire. But the average size of consolidated farms set up in three Ukrainian provinces west of the river Dnieper was nevertheless hardly massive: 15 acres (24:*586*). Most peasants in any case preferred the commune's guarantee of a degree of collective welfare, however inadequate, to the uncertainties of individual farming. In fact the Ministry of Agriculture relented its anti-communal drive before the Great War. It was finding that the 'consolidators' were often the most blatant exponents of soil-exhaustive methods since the pressure on them to make a quick profit was intense. By contrast, many communes welcomed advice on the introduction of multi-field crop rotations (86:*441,445*). But action through the commune involved settling for a much longer schedule for agricultural progress. Meanwhile, the climate still ruinously affected the harvest about once every seven years. And the soil quality in northern Russia meant that the region had to import grain and potatoes to subsist; and central Russia, which had traditionally exported its surplus thither in the previous century, failed to increase its output before the First World War as fast as the rise in its population (135:*6–7*).

Russian agriculture, then, was poised precariously between painstakingly won success and occasional utter ruin. The run of good harvests from 1909 to 1913 concealed the problems. Russian industry, too, faced dilemmas. The trough of 1905

21

and the ensuing recession was followed by sustained recovery aided vitally by an enormous French loan; and expansion continued through to the First World War. But again the appearance of unconditional advance, with the non-state civilian economy at last breaking clear of its past reliance upon governmental support, is misleading.

The state was having fewer miles of railway built, but governmental projects remained important as a fraction of overall industrial production: after the defeat in the Russo–Japanese war of 1904–5, involving the annihilation of the Baltic fleet, metallurgy received a much-needed boost from vast new defence orders (35:*105–7*). 'Rearmament' was not unique to Russia. But Germany, Britain and France were at a more advanced stage of industrialism. The deflection of investment away from non-military objectives surely had more adverse effects on those countries, notably Russia, whose transport network required to be very much denser than it presently was. The imperial government, furthermore, nurtured a cosy relationship with a small number of huge firms. Delivery on time and at fixed prices was judged to suit the state's interest better than laissez-faire competition. Scandals of excess profits recurred (68:*138*). It was unfortunate, too, that these metal-extractive and metal-processing companies were unable to satisfy the demand for agricultural implements. Imports of tools and machinery, particularly from the USA, expanded. Meanwhile many Russian firms not blessed with governmental contracts found the going hard. And, although the empire's industrial output increased before 1914, the still higher rate of increase in the USA and Germany meant that the gap in productive capacity was actually widening (5:*1104,1108*).

(x) Political instability

Of course, the real achievements in the economy are not to be understated. The dynamism of Russian agriculture and industry was impressive, and the strictly economic difficulties, in the factories if not in the countryside, posed no immediate basic threat to capitalist development. But the poverty of

22

nearly all workers and most peasants remained. Its persistence was a Damocles' sword hanging over the body of the imperial economy. From 1912, political travail returned.

Factory labourers intensified their struggle in that year. 2032 strikes broke out. The timing of the outburst was affected by the boom which had increased employment opportunities and allayed fears of confronting employers; and the long-standing grievances of working people had been made more acute by the changes introduced into factories to raise labour productivity after 1905 (49:*171*). The emphasis on 'scientific management' was not just a bosses' offensive (even though this was part of the story). Wages were low by the standards of western Europe; but labour overhead costs, measured in the provision of housing and training, were much higher (13:*404*). The pressure on industrialists to rationalise their operations was severe. The incipient crisis in labour relations was as much political as social: any lingering doubts about the regime's involvement on the bourgeoisie's side vanished with the shooting of workers on strike in the Lena goldfields in April 1912. The crescendo continued. In the first half of 1914 alone there were over 3000 strikes, and two-thirds of them were associated with political demands. The slogans were those espoused by the more intransigent Russian Marxists: both V. I. Lenin's Bolshevik faction and L. D. Trotski's supporters had cause for cheer (124:*191*). The police's penetration of all revolutionary groupings was as successful as ever; and presumably few workers were even acquainted with the doctrines of Bolshevism. Nonetheless the social unrest had reacquired political content. Huge demonstrations against the monarchy shook St Petersburg in summer 1914. The participants announced clear aims: they wanted a democratic republic, an eight-hour working day in the factories and the expropriation of all gentry-held land. And they wanted no delay of fulfilment (46:*365*).

The camarilla of court and government appeared incompetent and distasteful to larger and larger numbers of industrialists too. Nikolai II succumbed to autocratic recidivism. The base of his support became gravely narrow. Guchkov and some other Octobrists by 1913 were seeking to make an anti-governmental pact with the Kadets: moderate conservatism announced its despair of winning the emperor's sympathy (4:*122–3*). On the other hand, the monarchy's self-professed friends outside the Duma such as the proto-fascist Union Of The Russian People urged violently anti-constitutionalist policies which were manifestly outside the regime's powers to realise.

But events abroad superimposed themselves upon St Petersburg's political disarray. On 28 June 1914 the Austrian Archduke Franz Ferdinand was assassinated in Sarajevo, and the Austro-Hungarian government exploited the opportunity to provoke dispute with Serbia. Russia announced support for the Serbians. Austria-Hungary, encouraged by the German government, attacked Serbia. The Russian emperor began his army's preliminary mobilisation. Germany commenced to mobilise against Russia. France promised military solidarity with Russia, and a reluctant British cabinet backed the French move. By early August, the Great War engulfed Europe. The motives of each government were many, complex and controversial. In Russia, the crucial immediate decision to fight was taken by Nikolai II. He was concerned to preserve his country's prestige and its pretension to status as a Great Power. His upbringing and outlook inclined him to this reaction. Also of influence was the course of international relations. Around the turn of the century, St Petersburg and Berlin had settled their rivalries without undue difficulty. But Russia drew ever closer to her French ally after 1905 when loans raised in Paris proved vital to the autocracy. Germany's frustrations about her own global position grew in the same period. A Franco-German row over Morocco in 1905–6 resulted in Berlin's diplomatic defeat. On the other hand, Germany successfully sustained Austria-Hungary's annexation of Bosnia in 1908 despite Serbia's remonstrations. Russia had spoken in Serbia's favour, but the risk of war with Germany intimidated Nikolai II into climbing down. In 1914 he was unwilling to suffer another such humiliation. Probably he would have been goaded into a declaration of war, moreover, even if he had not declared it voluntarily. Conservative and liberal politicians in the Duma were equally alert to questions of national 'honour' and material interest (71:*69*). Economic as well as geo-political issues were at stake.

German industrial penetration of Russian markets was deepening. Many Russian factory and banking magnates looked forward to asserting themselves over a vanquished Germany, and several commercialists entertained the desire that Russia should hold the Straits of the Dardanelles. A few public figures even argued that a short, victorious war would terminate the tremors of revolution at home.

All such considerations came into play at court and in the Duma once the fateful entry into the war had been undertaken. The emperor's action was rapturously applauded. Worker and owner, peasant and landlord, civil servant, lawyer and aristocrat: all sections of the population joined in the patriotic enthusiasm. Anti-governmental strikes and demonstrations were abandoned. Optimism was in the ascendant. Certainly the Russian armed forces were not so dreadfully ill-prepared as was once supposed; indeed the German high command was fearful that Russian power would become insuperable unless a pre-emptive war were waged. But the first campaign in eastern Prussia was a massive set-back for Russia. At the battle of Tannenberg, in August 1914, the German army encircled the Russians and took hundreds of thousands of prisoners. It became clear, too, that the war would be a protracted affair. And the strains of all-out, lengthy warfare were bound to tell harder and harder on the Russian empire's economy and society. The point of political explosion moved nearer.

2   Explosion 1915–1917

Foreigners on Russian soil in 1917, with few exceptions, reported little else but chaos and carnage. Many welcomed the February Revolution but treated the October Revolution as the coming of Anti-Christ. How had it come about that the Bolsheviks could seize power in October? The answer widely proposed at the time and endorsed by countless commentators in our own day was unambiguous. The Bolshevik party manipulated an untutored public opinion among workers, soldiers and peasants. They grabbed governmental authority through conspiracy. They were disciplined and centralised, and they served their dictatorial leader Lenin with blind devotion. Thus the Russian 'masses' were highjacked into acceptance of the coup of October by a tiny, intellectual elite of megalomaniacs. The liberals and the moderate socialists had failed by dint of not acting forcefully enough and for not backing the army 'strong man', General Kornilov, who was prepared to strangle Bolshevism in its cradle.

(i) War and the gathering economic crisis

Undoubtedly much that happened in 1917 derived from the cunning of Bolshevik leaders and from the utopianism which sustained them and which they encouraged among working people. But the revolutionary explosion cannot be understood only in these terms. Economic conditions afford a starting-point. With the protraction of the fighting into 1915 (and, contrary to anti-tsarist propaganda, the Russian army acquitted itself quite adequately in the trenches) (121:*68*), the railways became overloaded and undermaintained. Priority was given to shipping conscripts, munitions and food to the Eastern front. Mining and metal-working enterprises, which were crucial to the army's fighting capacity, also secured favourable treatment. The rail network, barely able to cope with all its freight traffic in peacetime, in the war's first full year had trouble in getting sufficient grain from the south to the grain-deficient provinces of central and northern Russia (116:*7–8*). Urban rationing was already seriously contemplated. Good harvests in 1914 and 1915 were followed by a drop in cereal production in 1916 by 10 per cent below the annual average for the half-decade before the First World War (135:*3–5*). More wheat remained in the empire than before because Russian shipping had lost access to the Mediterranean; but the peasants were marketing less than had been customary. They were eating more, feeding more to livestock and turning more into illicit vodka.

The time and investment needed to repair and build up the railways was unavailable; and the higher prices necessary to tempt the peasantry to sell a greater quantity of its grain-stores could not be afforded by a government which had to commit its capital chiefly to the army in the trenches and to the armaments factories. Instant solutions did not exist. The state's stop-gap schemes included the raising of huge loans from its allies abroad and the printing of more rouble notes. Inflation resulted. The peasantry felt even less stimulus to engage in trade. A. A. Rittikh, the Minister of Agriculture, threatened to introduce a state levy of grain at fixed prices in November 1916, but the measure was unenforced through fear of antagonising the peasantry.

The industrial situation added to the problems. Production of agricultural implements crashed to 15 per cent of the pre-war level (141:*10*). There was little a peasant could buy even if he had a mind to. By 1916, 78 per cent of machine-construction business was given over to army requirements (79:*325*) By and large, industry satisfied the state's demands here. Factories in their hundreds adapted their plant and techniques to military work. Inevitably, output for the civilian market suffered. Partly this resulted from the greater attractiveness of the government's orders for shells, rifles and munitions. But not all enterprises obtained such contracts. And the problem for a firm not engaged in war-connected activity lay in getting hold of raw materials. The vast mining

27

cartel Prodamet, which was based in the Ukraine, could cause havoc for small and medium-sized firms simply by not selling them enough iron (which was the object of intense demand even before the war). The impaired condition of the railways compounded the difficulties. In 1915 there were the beginnings of a fuel and metal shortage. The talk by 1916 was of crisis. It was readily predictable that war manufacturing industries would also soon experience trouble.

To put all this down to the incompetence of the autocratic administration, as the regime's critics did and as some writers still do, is to exaggerate. A couple of years of war were bound to accentuate the defects of an economy not yet as modernised as that of its German foe; this would have occurred even if another political group, whether liberal or socialist, had been in charge of the war effort. Output and trade would undergo severe and increasing disruption so long as the state needed to keep millions of conscripts well-equipped and adequately fed. No change was likely while Russia remained in the Great War.

(ii) Social commotion

Such a situation nonetheless boded ill for the crown's hopes of obtaining popularity. The country's entry into the war led to a brief political lull; even many revolutionary activists shared in the general desire to defeat the Central Powers. But the economy's dislocation worsened the population's plight. Workers and garrison soldiers were going hungry. The size of the factory labour force increased as the defence industries expanded. By the end of 1916 there were nearly 3.5 million such labourers, and the conscription of perhaps as many as a quarter of the existing workingmen into the army meant that the influx into industrial employment was even more remarkable than it appeared to be (34:72,75). The pressure on housing stock was severe. St Petersburg, which was renamed Petrograd to give it a less Germanic resonance, was notorious for its squalid tenements. To be sure, real wages rose slightly in metal-working industries. In others, they declined (61:86–7; 77:89). And even a skilled metalworker, however much he

28

earned, could in any case only buy what groceries reached the shelves in the shops. Food retail turnover decreased sharply. Bread queues lengthened. Employers meanwhile intensified work routines, and the lack of proper maintenance standards made much machinery dangerous. Workers returned to seeking the regime's removal. Waves of strikes pounded official Russia in late 1915 and again in late 1916.

Labour unrest surged up in other combatant countries, but not on the same scale. Neither the British nor the German governments, moreover, had to navigate such storms of disaffection of the middle classes; not even the badly listing hulk of the Austro-Hungarian empire was yet being battered in this manner. Russia's 'free professions', such as medicine and education, found the state's bureaucratic structures still more irksome than before the war. Accounts of appalling underprovision of hospitals on the Eastern front grabbed headlines. Rasputin's intimacy with the empress Aleksandra offended everyone. Employers in industry, who had begun again to question the autocracy's aptitude for government before 1914, remained a divided group. Those with the profitable war contracts showed little disgruntlement. The base of their operations were the factories of Petrograd. But elsewhere the discontent was strong. In Moscow, many firms were either too small or too orientated upon civilian consumer production to gain a share in the wartime financial cake, and the opposition to the monarchy became entrenched among them (27:*30*). Thin cats wanted to be fat cats. Nor could Nikolai II count on much support even from the landed nobility. Its sons who served as army officers died thick and fast on the Eastern front, and the replacements in the trenches tended to be non-nobles who had less concern about the maintenance of the autocracy. Meanwhile the morale of the gentry in the countryside plumetted. Their economic well-being was direly menaced. The conscription of 14 million able-bodied young men reduced the number of mouths to be fed by the average peasant household, and this had the effect of eroding the financial pressure to seek work on capitalist-type estates or to pay high rents to the smaller landlords (58:*6*). Even the Council of the United Nobility toyed with favouring a change of regime by 1916 (87:*125–6*).

29

Yet the emperor and his series of premiers had never treated the Duma more contemptuously. Prorogation, and the threat of it, was the government's wartime sport; and Marxist deputies to the Fourth Duma who obstructed the vote on war credits were arrested. Police penetration of all the clandestine revolutionary parties was deep. But political opposition survived. Negotiations among anti-autocratic liberal and conservative groups inside the Duma yielded up an agreement to form a Progressive Bloc. Kadets, Octobrists and Progressists were at last getting together, and their unity facilitated the joint articulation of discontented professional, gentry and industrialist opinion. Humiliated in the Duma, they redoubled their efforts in the zemstva and various voluntary public bodies. The objective was to fill the gaps in the government's coverage of war services. Front hospitals were set up. Also influential were the War-Industry Committees. These were private institutions, established both at factory level and nationally, which had the regime's grudging permission to improve co-ordination in production and supply. Their existence came to be construed, however overstatedly, as proof of the authorities' administrative bankruptcy.

(iii) The February Revolution of 1917

Action, however, was not the Progressive Bloc's characteristic; thoughts of a coup scarcely turned to talk (with the exception of Octobrist leader Guchkov's soundings in December 1916). Liberals and conservatives worried that a revolution might lead to an eruption of the fury of the 'masses'. The workers' organisations were the monarchy's more dangerous adversaries. Not a few industrialists thought it impolitic to go on allowing the factory workforces to send representatives to the War-Industry Committees; and the sick-funds were being used by revolutionaries to encourage political unrest (78:*372–3*). The government vigorously suppressed strikes in late 1916. Its nerve seemed unbreakable: a revolt in central Asia by Moslems unwilling to be conscripted was brutally quelled. But the regime's power was in fact weakening. Workers remained the vanguard of the opposition. In February 1917,

30

trouble broke out in the Putilov arms works. Women textile labourers went on strike. Demonstrations filled the capital's thoroughfares. The Petrograd garrison mutinied. The emperor's appeal to front-line headquarters for armed intervention was made too late and indecisively; in any event, the disenchantment with the monarch had by then spread even to the high command. No civilian or military group wanted autocracy preserved.

On 2 March, a bewildered Nikolai II agreed to abdicate. Pressure to do so had ultimately been applied by an unofficial group of politicians from the Duma, and these proceeded to form a Provisional Government. Adherents of the Progressive Bloc predominated in the cabinet. A majority were Kadets. They moved swiftly to promulgate civic freedoms of speech, assembly and association and promised to hold elections, with a universal-adult franchise, to a Constituent Assembly. They aimed to keep Russia in the war. But they refrained from adverting attention to their objective to fight on for all-out victory and territorial gain. They refused, too, to initiate agrarian reform. They wanted the land question to be held over for resolution by the Constituent Assembly. A concern for procedural niceties is evident here. But the Kadets were also reasoning pragmatically; their argument was that, if they decreed a transfer of all land to the peasantry, the resultant turmoil would disrupt agricultural activity and disorganise the army (since peasant conscripts would desert to their villages to acquire their share of the local landowner's estate) (107:*127–8*). In addition, the Kadets did what they could to prevail upon the workers' organisations to exercise self-restraint in their bargaining with employers. They stressed that military security would suffer severe damage if industrial disputes dragged on. Such judgements were corollaries of the Provisional Government's goals in the war. But they entailed an abstention from earlier social radicalism. Kadets in 1905 had drawn up a plan for the compulsory dispossession of the nobility's landed property, albeit with financial compensation. For some years they had been less keen to highlight schemes of this sort. Their adhesion to the Progressive Bloc in 1915 had signalled the Kadets' intuition that, to preserve any hope of attaining authority, they would have to throw in their

31

lot with Russia's proprietorial elite. Their trepidation about workers and peasants had only been aggravated by the February events. To say the least, there was a lack of urgency about their arrangements to put their mandate to govern to the test of Constituent Assembly elections.

Thus the physiognomy of the Kadets as the catch-all party for the protection of urban and rural middle-class interests was no accident, and even industrialists who had profited from close links with the old regime happily started to support the Provisional Government: and few among the reactionary die-hards of the gentry actively opposed the Kadet-led administration.

Yet the writing was already on the wall. In setting up their cabinet, the Kadets and their allies had to maintain amicable relations with a mass organisation thrown up in the course of the February Revolution: the Petrograd Soviet. Premier G. E. Lvov owed his elevation not only to liberal pressure upon the emperor to abdicate but also to the Soviet's acquiescence. 'Dual power' was built into the post-revolutionary settlement. The uneasy symbiosis of Government and Soviet in the capital had its parallels across the country as workers and soldiers (and, though not so quickly, peasants) established a profusion of soviets and other sectional mass organisations. If anything, the fragility of the governmental apparatus was greater in the provinces. The cabinet dismissed the old governors. It appointed its own commissars instead, and these were to work in consort with the various 'committees of public safety' which had sprung up to welcome the monarchy's overthrow and which were usually led by liberals (138:*11–13*). Such bodies were not long-lasting. A resurgence of the municipal councils and the zemstva was officially heralded. But these had to be re-elected for the first time on an unrestricted franchise, and the Kadets ran into electoral reverses. Problems were great in Russia and greater still in the non-Russian regions. The Provisional Government's reluctance to grant more than limited autonomy to local representative institutions aroused hostility in the Ukraine and Finland. Throughout the country, moreover, state power was paltry. The police had been disbanded in the February upheaval, and the garrison soldiers were treated warily by the Lvov cabinet. The Church was no friend of the Kadets. Clerics anyway participated little in public life. Freed from centuries of governmental tutelage, they were intoxicated by their liberty to engage in strife among themselves.

The gap between the government and popular opinion, however, was as yet a crack and not a chasm. The workers with their street demonstrations and fighting had brought down Nikolai the Bloody, and yet they stood aside as a 'bourgeois' cabinet assumed power. Some Bolsheviks felt that a socialist government should have been created instantly; this had been their intended strategy since 1905 (111:*78*).

(iv) Aspirations in society

Workers in general had not thought in such terms. They knew of their numerical weakness in relation to the rest of the country, and believed in the need for national unity. The last thing they wanted was a civil war (73:*82*). Their political aspirations were still in the course of formation; but probably, as before the Great War, they desired a democratic republic, an eight-hour working day and higher wages (31:*154*). They apparently rejected the objective of territorial expansion in the War. Defence was their goal (61:*241*) In the February Revolution's first days the workers were already proving their determination. Dignified treatment at work was demanded. Obnoxious managers and foremen were roughed up; sometimes they were daubed with red paint or tossed in a sack, and were carted round the factory in a wheelbarrow (and occasionally the worst of them were thrown into rivers). Such humiliating behaviour was designed to indicate that no future humiliation of working people was going to be tolerated (117:*55–7*). These ructions also supplied power to the thrust towards a raising of wages. Initially employers responded threateningly. The tradition of preferring attack to cautious concession had not wilted. But the workers held firm, and the settlements reached in spring led to rises in real wages and to more relaxed methods of handling disputes.

Civil servants and members of the professions gave much less trouble. Support for the Kadets was strong among them;

and the Provisional Government, after sacking the provincial governors and officials in the Ministry of Internal Affairs, left the state bureaucracy intact. Working protocol was eased. Experts warmed to the greater appreciation of their expertise. Yet other agencies were more hostile. Most army and navy officers accepted the new cabinet without demur, but the troops were less easily satisfied. Killings of notorious martinets occurred in February (76:*14*). Soldiers in the Petrograd garrison prodded the Soviet into issuing Order No. 1. They would no longer salute officers off-duty, they wanted to be addressed in polite language. Above all, they claimed the right to elect their own committees to protect their interests. The Provisional Government came to terms, and the reforms were extended to the rest of the armed forces. Troops in the garrisons were more aggressive politically than those at the front. Yet all conscripts welcomed the concessions. Allegiance to the government was sworn. But soldiers in general increasingly indicated that their loyalty depended upon the authorities convoking a Constituent Assembly, restricting military operations to defence and genuinely seeking to negotiate a continental peace (139:*287,321*).

Such a development was unparalleled in the armies of the other combatant countries, and it restricted the cabinet's scope of action severely. Ministers, however, continued to talk confidently. They were pleased that at least the countryside had been tranquil in the days of the February Revolution. The peasants in uniform, as most soldiers were, gave more overt sign of restlessness than did their families and neighbours back in the villages. But this quietude was temporary. A profound impatience pervaded the peasantry too, and the Provisional Government's postponement of fundamental land reform alienated the rural millions. Peasants had for centuries believed that the land should belong only to those who worked on it; and most of them, though by no means all, desired that the commune should direct such a transformation. Half-measures were not going to placate them. Some negotiations with landlords were friendly and peaceful in March 1917, but violence also occurred. In the same month 183 disturbances were reported in the ethnically Russian provinces of the old empire (65:*88*); 49 cases of arson were registered (79:*848*).

The peasantry was acting within historical character; it had customarily put up with its lot for decades and then suddenly, when an externally provoked crisis affected the villages, risen up in pursuit of particular ends. Its lack of political sophistication in no way diminished its menace to the post-autocratic order. It wanted the land, and in 1917 it at last had the perfect opportunity to take it.

(v) 'Dual power'

In this situation the government cast round for any agency capable of controlling political radicalism. They found what they thought they needed in the soviet leadership. Two socialist parties, the Mensheviks and the Socialist Revolutionaries, held the soviets by virtue of having attracted the most votes in the first elections. Both were willing to accept the Provisional Government so long as it protected the gains in civic freedoms and fought only a defensive war against Germany; the Provisional Government, for its part, hoped that these parties would dissuade workers, peasants and soldiers from demanding too much.

Such a compromise initially gave some grounds for optimism. The Mensheviks, who had totalled a handful of thousands before February 1917, quickly became a mass party after the February Revolution and by autumn had about 200,000 members (67:*389*). The Socialist-Revolutionaries recruited in the countryside as well as in the towns and, with a vaunted figure of 1 million members (93:*236*), were easily the largest party. Neither the Mensheviks nor the Socialist-Revolutionaries yet wanted governmental office. Of course, they had their programmatic disagreements. The Mensheviks as conventional Marxists of their time assigned the leading role to the urban working class in the eventual achievement of socialism, and they admired large-scale, centralised forms of organisation in state and society. The Socialist-Revolutionaries, following traditions of Russian populism, extolled small-scale and decentralised organisational arrangements. They refused to let the positive potentiality of the peasantry be ignored. Even so, a substantial convergence of

35

the two viewpoints had for several years been observable. The Socialist-Revolutionaries' ascendant leaders, unlike the populists of the 1870s but like the Mensheviks in their own day, considered that the Russian industrial economy required further capitalist development, so as to build up the country's productive strength and cultural resources, before socialists should try to assume power (48:*105–8*). In any case, the Socialist-Revolutionaries aimed at a revolution by and for all 'the toiling people' (and not just the peasantry) (88:*80–1*). And, more immediately, both parties judged that wartime was the most unpropitious situation for going it alone and risking economic catastrophe through a break with the bourgeoisie (128:*245,312*).

Their conditional support for the Provisional Government was a logical consequence. But it involved turning a blind eye. They avoided seeing that the Kadets had expansionist war aims. In April this could no longer be ignored. Foreign Minister Pavel Milyukov notified London and Paris that the Provisional Government stood by the terms of the treaty arrangements of 1915. The Mensheviks and Socialist-Revolutionaries in the Petrograd Soviet organised a demonstration in protest. The existence of 'dual power' was emphasised: the Lvov cabinet met in panic, and Milyukov and Guchkov resigned.

The need for an institutional framework of liaison with Mensheviks and Socialist-Revolutionaries was the lesson now drawn by the Kadets. Lvov invited the Petrograd Soviet to supply representatives to join a coalition. Reluctantly the Soviet's Executive Committee complied. From May 1917, the ministerial set-up included a minority of socialists; their most energetic men were the Mensheviks I. G. Tsereteli and M. I. Skobelev and the Socialist-Revolutionary V. M. Chernov. The tug-of-war inside the governmental coalition was fierce. It is unfair to maintain that the incoming ministers put up no resistance to Kadet policies. Tsereteli worked to convoke a conference of socialist parties from all combatant countries in neutral Sweden with the purpose of exerting non-violent pressure on all governments to terminate the war. Skobelev introduced measures for the improvement of factory workers' welfare and for the increased state regulation of industry (and this in turn provoked the resignation of the Progressist A. I. Konovalov) (106:*130*). Chernov opposed the government's refusal to effect agrarian reform; and, disregarding the cabinet's haverings, he let it be known that he approved the rapid transfer of all agricultural soil to the peasantry through the channels of locally elected land committees (39:*102–3*). Yet these campaigns, while not cosmetic, had slight effect. The Stockholm Conference never met, and Skobelev's measures scarcely infringed the private interest in the Russian industrial economy. As for the land question, Chernov's fiery statements outside the Provisional Government's rooms in the Tauride Palace were a symptom of his impotence to change policy within them.

The conclusion must be that the Kadets were winning the contest. Their triumph derived largely from their competitors-cum-colleagues' conviction that they themselves should not yet be holding power. Mensheviks and Socialist-Revolutionaries, moreover, retained a fear that the acutest threat to 'the Revolution' came from the political right; the possibility of a military coup was never far from their thoughts (106:*161*). This was another stimulus for them to hug close to the Kadets as being lesser demons than a dictator from the army. Kadet politicians spotted their chances. In June 1917 the cabinet ordered the opening of an offensive on the Eastern front. The Austrian sector, in Galicia, was attacked. A short advance prefaced a long retreat. The Austrians called in German reinforcements, and the Russian General Brusilov's forces ended up digging new trenches in the Ukraine to stabilise the frontline.

(vi) Economic breakdown and social reactions

Events at the summit of the Russian state were in any case like a sub-plot in the main drama of 1917. The working class as well as the peasantry in army and countryside were actors in their own history. Politicians everywhere talked of the clashes between the 'centre' and the 'localities' between 'the top' and 'the bottom', between the 'authorities' and the 'elemental masses'; it all seemed so topsy-turvy, even unnatural to most of them. Only one major party, the Bolsheviks, welcomed the phenomenon. Workers thought over their approach in the light of their current experiences and, because mutual antipathy had always separated them from the Russia of property and power, their reaction to the deterioration of output and supplies was firm and unequivocal. Industry's decline continued. It is suggested that profit margins in heavy-manufacturing factories, while falling to almost half of their level in 1916, were nevertheless at around 9 per cent (which was in fact slightly higher than the pre-war average) (129:*281*). But this figure presumably refers only to enterprises which stayed operational throughout 1917, and it tells us nothing about the light-industrial sector. A truer index of the plight of manufacturing, both heavy and light, is the fall-off in monthly coal output by 27 per cent between January and August 1917 (129:*289*). In addition, factories across the country as early as April were reckoned to be receiving less than two-fifths of the metal needed for the fulfilment of contracts (129:*185*). Inflation accelerated. Transport difficulties increased. Closures of enterprises began. And food supplies to the towns worsened. A state monopoly in the trade of grain was proclaimed in March alongside measures to introduce urban rationing of bread; but the norms could not be held to, and cuts were made successively in April and June (129:*457*). The wage settlements, furthermore, failed to keep up with the rise in prices (61:*132*).

The bloody-mindedness of employers towards factory workers was no myth, and the textile millionaire Ryabushinski was not alone in praying that 'the bony hand of hunger' would constrain the workforce to moderate their aspirations. But industry would have been prone to collapse even if the mutual distrust of owners and workers had disappeared. The shortage of capital and raw materials was being noted before the February Revolution; industrial disputes merely worsened an already worsening situation. The urban working class glimpsed a winter of starvation as a distinct possibility. Strikes still took place, but their effectiveness was small at a time when employers were cutting back on production. Self-maintenance in a job in a working factory became the pressing need. This increased the workforce's militancy, and the regular mass meetings inside the gates of the enterprise convinced many industrialists that labour productivity would continue to fall. Workers, on their side, were determined never to be done down again. They developed a solidarity between their skilled and unskilled sections, including women, born out of the common threat to their livelihood (117:*198–9*); they were united, too, by the belief that a fairer world than that of capitalism could be constructed. Their elected factory committees were empowered by them to supplant the existing management if closure seemed imminent. 'Workers' control' became a rallying cry. The first implementation of such schemes occurred in Petrograd in midsummer.

The origins of this movement were defensive; mindless aggressiveness was not widespread (even though it must be added that the workers' chances of staving off the industrial collapse itself were slim in the extreme). The disaffection of soldiers, especially in the garrisons, had a similar basis. The June offensive on the Austro-Hungarian frontal sector demonstrated the Kadets' will to win the war, and the thought of being used as cannon fodder alarmed more and more troops. Desertions had not yet become a massive problem in July and August. But distrust of the governmental authorities was widespread. The fact that not even the daily arrival of food could be guaranteed instigated further discontent. The soldiers' and sailors' attitude was in itself disturbing. Yet it provoked other worries in the cabinet too; the lack of a dependable military force meant that nothing could restrain the peasants from doing as they liked. In fact the official procurement agencies in the eight months of the Provisional Government's existence failed by less than 1½ per cent to equal the amount of grain bought by Nikolai II's bureaucrats in the last eight months of the old regime. The drawback was that this was only 48 per cent of recognised national requirements (129:*442–3*). In desperation, the government doubled its fixed agricultural prices in August. No steady improvement resulted (129:*431,442*). Nor was the peasantry's opposition merely passive. Land seizures became frequent: the government's declaration that the Constituent Assembly alone should decide the agrarian question was spitting into the wind. Meadows were an early peasant objective; three-fifths of

39

occupations of pastures took place in June and July. Arable land, apparently, was seized at a more stable rate from May through to October. Mere residence by landowners was treated as resistance. Killings occurred. Violence in general was plentiful; at the peak of the trouble, in July, 481 'disturbances' were reported (39:*204*).

(vii) Mass organisations

Land communes, at least in most of European Russia, co-ordinated such activity just as factory committees did in the towns. Their impact was not some exclusive magical feat of the Bolsheviks. Few villages saw any of the party's agitators, and fewer still had a resident Bolshevik group. Most towns acquired a party committee. Even so, a shortage of experienced manpower was a constant complaint of Bolsheviks in the provinces. Consequently opponents of the party who attributed revolutionism predominantly to a malign, ubiquitous Bolshevism were overstating the case. Workers and peasants were switching political attitudes without much prodding from Lenin and his comrades. Equally exaggerated was the charge that all would have been sweetness and light if only 'the intelligentsia' had not led 'the masses' by the nose. That is not to say that middle-class activists were without influence. In the local soviets their skills were at a premium (54:*116*); and at the national level, in Petrograd, intellectuals were especially prominent. But they were a divided stratum. Some, like Lenin and Trotski, were fiery Bolsheviks; others such as Tsereteli belonged to socialist parties which tried to restrain the working class from direct action on the streets. In addition, ex-workers were among the leading soviet politicians. The Menshevik K. Gvozdev was a key figure. And the incidence of middle-class leaders was probably very slight in the factory committees (117:*190–1*). Possibly it was not much greater in local trade union branches. The various mass organisations showed that working people could mobilise themselves with some vigour in protection of their interests.

Indeed the monarchy's overthrow had allowed the entire population, from the nobility through to the workers, to join in the democratic enthusiasm. Sectional bodies abounded. Electing, debating and demanding became a regular activity. Governmental power remained frail. Indeed the soviets became a potential alternative government. They held their first national congress in June. It in turn chose an All-Russian Central Executive Committee to conduct business until the next congress. Mensheviks and Socialist-Revolutionaries retained their majority, and their representatives in the Petrograd Soviet were transferred to posts in the national soviet apparatus. Commissions were created to keep watch on the ministries of the Provisional Government. These were hectic times. The Central Executive Committee, with its dozens of members, was too unwieldy to allow for rapid response to sudden changes in circumstance. Authority was devolved to an inner Presidium (and, eventually, to a core of prominent officials such as Tsereteli who were dubbed the 'Star Chamber'). Kadet ministers were alarmed by the consolidation of the central soviet machine as well as by their own ineffectualness in imposing governmental decrees on the country. They desired to frighten the Mensheviks and Socialist-Revolutionaries into firmer support for them, and resigned from the cabinet *en masse* in the first week of July. Hurried consultations followed. A second coalition was formed; A. F. Kerenski, nominally a Socialist-Revolutionary party member since the February Revolution, became premier and put together a Provisional Government with a majority for the moderate socialists from the soviets and with only four Kadets.

On the face of it, the Mensheviks and the Socialist-Revolutionaries had taken power by stealth. Yet the reality was different. Kerenski's policies contrasted little with those of the Kadets except in rhetoric. The Provisional Government's record, however, has attracted much casual disdain. The consideration ought to be kept in mind that the moderate socialists were not endeavouring to accomplish something outlandish. What was Ramsay MacDonald's National Government of 1931 in Great Britain but a similar attempt to prevent economic collapse by unifying political groups on the right and left? The analogy should not be pressed too hard. Suffice it to add that nothing had occurred since the February

Revolution to jolt most Mensheviks or Socialist-Revolutionaries into thinking Russia ready for socialism. If anything, events seemed to them to confirm their scepticism. Economic ruin and military setbacks continued. Then there were the increasing signs of social disorder; Chernov himself was nearly lynched by workers and sailors in Petrograd in July. A final struggle to achieve a reconciliation of all classes appeared appropriate.

Thus the central soviet leaders, while looking as if they had ensconced a socialist administration, shuddered at the very notion. They studiously avoided giving great offence to the Kadets; and this meant that an alternative government, if it was to be established, had to be initiated from another source. This occurred in the provinces. Slowly in summer 1917, like blank photographic paper revealing its image in a developing bath, a political revolution was beginning to manifest itself. Not all town soviets across the country were as diffident as the Central Executive Committee in the capital; those in Kronstadt and Tsaritsyn, being bitterly opposed to the Provisional Government, were with difficulty dissuaded from declaring themselves as independent republics (38:*96–7*; 95:*207*). Others were less hostile. But they tended nonetheless to supplant the official bureaucracy in several normal governmental functions. They set up militias to police their area. They provided food kitchens and educational facilities. They held festivals. Their word could countermand orders given by garrison commanders; they could intervene directly in the life of the economy in their locality. This development was not confined to Russia. Outlying cities, like Baku on the Caspian, evolved similarly (122:*119,131*). Menshevik and Socialist-Revolutionary leaderships in the town soviets away from the capital had willy-nilly been drawn into encroaching upon the prerogatives of the local agencies of the Provisional Government. Where they held back, the suburb soviets often pushed in and did the job instead. The overall trend was for lower soviet bodies to ignore their hierarchical superiors whenever conflicts over substantive politics arose (131:*235*).

This explains why workers, soldiers and peasants exhibited so great a faith in 'the soviets' and 'soviet power' even though the Central Executive Committee refused to accede to their demands for more radical reforms in the economy and society. Mass participation in the discussions in the soviets continued through 1917. The open meetings supplied a forum for popular opinion to be voiced, and plenary sessions of soviet deputies were seldom held in camera. Deputies could be individually recalled for failing to represent the constituency's wishes. Admittedly, the system was prone to abuse: executive committee sessions became less well attended; general elections of soviets were held at longer intervals; functionaries acquired over-authoritative modes of dealing with their constituents (54:*124–6*). By and large, however, local soviet bodies were responsive to requests from below. They recognised that this was the *sine qua non* of their authority in such a tumultuous environment. The clearest warning came from the workers. In spring 1917, many soviets tried to temper working-class aspirations; the factory labour force countered by playing institutional leap-frog: they jumped across to other mass organisations such as the factory committees to seek satisfaction (117:*179–81*).

(viii) The Bolshevik Party

The fluidity of such politics was bewildering. It placed a requirement upon all parties to react swiftly, sensitively and decisively. Only the Bolsheviks achieved this. Their success was intimately connected with the fact that they were the only major party unconditionally hostile to the Provisional Government. Their standpoint was clear by April. They wanted the government to be overthrown and replaced by an administrative structure based upon the soviets. They wavered a little; they dropped the slogan 'All Power To The Soviets' in late summer when their prospects of enhancing their position in the soviets seemed poor. But the abandonment was temporary. On the war, moreover, Bolshevik policy was constant. They aimed at an immediate general peace. They argued that a socialist revolution in Russia would spark off revolutions in Germany and elsewhere, and that these would put an end to the fighting without annexations or indemnities. They called for national self-determination in the former Russian empire

43

and throughout the world. Their economic objectives at home included governmental ownership of the large industrial firms and all the banks. Land nationalisation was another intention; it was expected to take the form mainly of the peasantry seizing non-peasant fields and cultivating them for private profit. The Bolsheviks would hold the Constituent Assembly elections. They confidently predicted a victory which would justify the taking of power by the soviets (which, as sectional institutions, usually denied representation to the middle and upper social classes). This projected dictatorship involved a modification of strategy. Until 1917, Bolsheviks had expected autocracy's demise to be followed by a lengthy epoch of rule by bourgeoisie. Now they wanted to commence the transition to socialism without delay. The party leader Vladimir Lenin expressed these ideas in his *April Theses*. And, on his return from Switzerland, he gladly noted that many Bolsheviks had independently come to the same broad conclusion. The April Party Conference witnessed a triumph of the new line (112:*46,53–4*).

The Bolshevik party was loosely structured. The formal rules demanded that rank-and file members, activists, officials and lower party bodies should obey higher bodies. But neither Lenin nor the Central Committee could automatically secure submission. Persuasion counted for a great deal. Equally decisive was the agreement of nearly all Bolsheviks about the key immediate goals. This consensus was in embryo in March. Opposition was at its strongest in the Central Committee but was quickly surmounted; at lower levels, those party members who objected left the Bolsheviks (112:*49*). The process had its traumas. Thousands of rank-and-filers remained hostile to the division of the Bolsheviks and Mensheviks into separate parties; but, by midsummer, such inhibitions had evaporated because of disgust with Menshevik collaboration with the Kadets. The road was open for the consolidation of an anti-war, pro-revolution mass party; and the Bolsheviks grasped the opportunity. A few thousand persons considered themselves Bolsheviks in February 1917. By late summer it was being claimed, with some exaggeration, that the figure had soared to a quarter of a million. The influx was not confined to rank-and-filers. Merely 83 per cent of Party Congress delegates in July 1917, according to an official questionnaire, had been Bolsheviks before the First World War (and perhaps 23 per cent had previously adhered to the Mensheviks or other parties) (112:*43,49*).

What made this party so dynamic an agency of revolutionism was not its mutterings of dogma. Nor was it just Lenin's tactical genius. On the contrary, his judgement was sometimes badly awry (92:*310–12*). In mid-June, he encouraged the holding of an armed demonstration of workers and sailors against the Provisional Government; it was only at the last moment, in the first week of July, that he recognised his impetuosity and tried to call it all off. The postponement came too late. Troops fired on the demonstrators. Prominent Bolsheviks, including Lenin, were ordered to be arrested. He himself escaped to Finland. Yet the fiasco of his intervention was less important on this occasion than the evidence that ever larger numbers in the factories and garrisons favoured policies of direct political action. The party and the working class were not neatly discrete entities. Workers constituted around three-fifths of the membership in late 1917 (112:*43–4*), and this enabled local committees to stay in touch with popular mood as it developed. Local issues were often as important as those of national significance in Bolshevik party campaigns. Not infrequently the so-called 'party masses' pushed their committees towards more radical measures. The attitude was fierce and exalted and, as material conditions worsened, a little desperate too. Highly 'democratic' and highly 'authoritarian' ideas co-existed in Bolshevik thought; and party members at all levels, even in the Central Committee, felt under little obligation to resolve the contradictions of their future policies in advance. There was a belief that 'practice' would fill in the lacunae of 'theory'. This optimism was misplaced, but it did no harm to the party's drive for recruits and electoral backing. The Bolsheviks came to seem very attractive by virtue of being the only group which truly believed that the horrendous difficulties of war and economy and government were immediately surmountable.

(ix) The disintegration of the state

The polarisation of Russian politics proceeded relentlessly; and, as the Bolsheviks' popularity in the towns increased, so did their representation in the various mass organisations. First factory committees and then, not long afterwards, soviets came under their influence. Petrograd, Kronstadt and Tsaritsyn were areas of early success. That this could be happening by September was a tribute to the party's resilience. The arrests of Trotski and Kollontai in the capital and the flight of Lenin and Zinoviev to the Finnish marshes were accompanied by a campaign of vilification in the press. But these were minor setbacks. Bolshevism had always claimed to be the people's bulwark against counter-revolution, and Kerenski could not repulse the forces of the far right without their assistance. Kerenski's manoeuvres were of labyrinthine obscurity. In order to reassert the Provisional Government's authority in Petrograd, in August he ordered Commander-in-Chief L. G. Kornilov to transfer combat troops to the capital. At the last moment he suspected Kornilov of intending a coup d'état. Kornilov, meeting the threat of his own arrest, concluded that a coup was indeed desirable as Kerenski was not going to batter the unruly soviets after all. Bolshevik as well as Socialist-Revolutionary and Menshevik activists hastened out to persuade Kornilov's units to disobey their commander. No armed might of the Petrograd garrison would have stopped him. The mission succeeded, and Kornilov was placed under house detention. The Bolsheviks then renewed the political struggle without even the harassments from the government that had bothered them since July (92:*158–9*).

Fortune was with them for the while. There was little chance of conscripts wanting to join anti-socialist brigades like the Freikorps which marauded German cities from late 1918. The Provisional Government had no such contingents at its disposal. It also faced resistance even in regions where the Bolshevik party lacked strength. Anti-Russian feelings grew throughout the old empire. The Ukraine was becoming ungovernable from Petrograd; its own elected *Rada* held Kiev. Armenians, Azeris and Georgians sought greater freedom (125:*96–7*). Liberty for Finland was demanded. What is more, politics were not only mainly non-violent but also sealed off from direct foreign intervention. The British and French armies were engaged in the man-hungry battles in the West. The Americans had joined the Allies in spring 1917 after

German attacks on their shipping, but their troops did not arrive in France until 1918.

Meanwhile the Allies' ties to the Provisional Government did it nothing but harm. There had been the disastrous resumption of offensives on the Eastern front in late June; with Russian military weakness exposed for the world to see, the British and French cabinets completed the humiliation by extruding Kerenski's diplomats from discussions on the post-war territorial arrangements to be made in the Balkans (139:*98,100*). The government's helplessness was still more cruelly exposed when, in August, the German army smashed through the defences on the Baltic littoral and took Riga. Any further advance would have jeopardised Petrograd too. Kerenski was compelled to hearken more attentively to the desires of his Menshevik and Socialist-Revolutionary contacts. The Kadets were cool towards him in August when he summoned a 'State Conference' in Moscow to assist all parties and public organisations, from the far right through to the far left, in getting together to deliberate on the country's travail; they resigned again from the government on the eve of Kornilov's putsch (107:*229*). In panic he convoked a Democratic Conference in September. This event was arranged on a narrower basis; not only the far right but also the liberals, whose tacit condoning of Kornilov scandalised all socialist opinion, were discouraged from being present. But the results were not constructive. An agreement was made to move faster in the direction of the policies pushed by Tsereteli and Chernov in the first coalition cabinet, and to form a cabinet without the Kadets. But tamer thoughts prevailed. Kerenski wanted Kadets in his team, and some proved willing to join it (107:*244–6*).

(x) The October Revolution of 1917

The Bolsheviks treated the Democratic Conference with contempt, and they attended it only long enough to declare the need for a socialist programme, and then left. The danger of moving too fast was recognised by their Central Committee. They wisely cast aside Lenin's counsel to seize power without

47

further ado. They went on building up their base in the soviet infrastructure while the frantic Kerenski's authority shrank daily. The expectation of a Bolshevik seizure of power grew. The blithe hope was nurtured, by groups from the Kadets through to unashamed monarchists, that Lenin's party would quickly be crippled by the onus of office.

Nor were all Bolsheviks yet convinced that a favourable moment had arrived. Lenin, however, lunged back into the reckoning. He had limitless capacity to persuade, cajole and goad. On 10 October, the Central Committee debated the question of state power. Lenin returned clandestinely from Finland to participate, and the consequent decision came from his pen. Still he had to be restrained. He wanted power seized immediately. Trotski's view was preferred, that the uprising should be timed to allow state authority to be grasped on the opening day of the Second All-Russian Congress of Soviets. Thus 'soviet power' would be established. Even so, there was uncertainty about the strength of active support for the Bolsheviks in Petrograd. Even many leftists in the party reported on workers' lack of enthusiasm for violent measures. But organised, adequate forces were forthcoming. The Petrograd Soviet, through its Military-Revolutionary Committee, controlled the garrison; and workers in the Red Guard had the necessary arms and commitment. These overwhelmed the government's guard at the Winter Palace. At all events, popular uprisings have never been organised by a people as a whole. Only a minority directly participates. And, by mid October, Lenin could also argue that soviets in city after city throughout Russia were following the example of Petrograd and Moscow in acquiring Bolshevik majorities. The Second Soviet Congress would undoubtedly put the party in charge of the central soviet apparatus. Working-class opinion had swung in favour of Kerenski's removal; and it seemed as if the trend was irreversible, especially as the Bolsheviks were willing to adjust policies to take account of demands from the factories: the adoption of the slogan of 'workers' control' in May 1917 was a vivid example (117:155). The bid for peasant support was raised too. Lenin, recognising rural suspicions of his land nationalisation proposal, declared instead that the land should become the property of 'the entire people'.

48

The February Revolution was in the final stages of decay, and some kind of socialist government would very likely have emerged from the chaos in any case; it was Lenin's initiative that ensured that this government took the form it did. The transfer of power in Petrograd was not attended by lengthy conflict. The City Soviet's Military-Revolutionary Committee, directed by Trotski, acted efficiently. On 25 October 1917 the Provisional Government was disbanded and authority was assumed by the All-Russian Congress of Soviets.

3 The Limits of Experiment, 1917–1927

The outside world could make little sense of the October Revolution in its early years. Even the spelling of 'Bolsheviks' gave trouble. The meteoric passage of Lenin's party from the shadows of pre-1917 clandestinity to power and renown in Petrograd baffled and, except among groups of the political far left, terrified those seeking to understand it. Wartime disruption of communications impeded analysis. Another problem was that the Bolsheviks said they were socialists and yet, unmistakably, they differed basically from most socialists in countries to the West. Fantastic stories gained currency. A vogue grew up for the traveller's tale of depravity and torture. The Bolsheviks supposedly had descended upon Russia like a new Mongol horde; but, unlike Genghis Khan, they were held to be pursuing a meticulously articulated grand plan. Alas for Mother Russia! The Bolshevik Central Committee was deemed to have pre-ordained for her a nightmare of social engineering. The assumption was rife that Lenin and his associates had already determined exactly how and when to realise their objective. Russia was to be the first experimental grist in the Bolshevik mill. The rest of the globe would shortly follow.

(i) Political euphoria

It is idle to deny that Bolshevism had snatched the helm of government with several definite ideas about the course to be steered, or that leading Bolsheviks found it abhorrent to use massive violence. Yet the party did not come to power with an all-embracing, long-term Plan. Its detailed expressions of

50

intent bore upon issues of the moment; and its thinking, while in some ways showing exceptional practicality, was extremely light-headed in others.

The promulgation of policies began on the morrow of the seizure of power. The Second Congress of Soviets, with its predominance of Bolsheviks, installed a Bolshevik government. Its name, as abbreviated in Russian, was Sovnarkom; its fuller version in translation was the Council of People's Commissars. The premier, or 'chairman', was Lenin. The expectation was that revolutions would break out across Europe within days. A decree on peace was published. It called for an instant end to the war without annexations or indemnities. The right of national self-determination was proclaimed, and Poland (which was anyway under German occupation) and Finland were granted independence. Bolsheviks called on workers and soldiers abroad to overthrow their governments. Political harmony and economic reconstruction and advance were predicted for the entire continent. Meanwhile the party would not wait upon events. The months after October saw the nationalisation of several large factories and of all the banks. Foreign trade was placed under governmental supervision. Sovnarkom unilaterally annulled the debts of Nikolai II's and Kerenski's administrations. 'Workers' control' was announced in industry. Labourers in each enterprise were authorised to keep a check on their managers. A reversal of industrial decline was anticipated. This in turn was deemed certain to put the exchange of commodities between town and countryside in motion again. Peasant support was vital. The Bolsheviks wanted an alliance of the proletariat and the poorer peasants. A decree on land was issued. Local peasant soviets were instructed to oversee the redistribution of the estates of crown, church and nobility. All non-peasant land was declared expropriated without compensation.

On 25 October, soviet power extended little beyond Petrograd. But Kerenski's attempted counter-coup with mounted Cossacks was a charade, and the City Soviet acted through its Military-Revolutionary Committee to secure the capital for the new administration (102:51–2). The Bolshevik-led soviets in other towns followed suit. In northern and central Russia this was mostly a painless process. Fighting lasted several

51

days in Moscow. In Ivanovo-Voznesensk the worst commotion was an uproarious rendition of the 'Internationale' to celebrate Sovnarkom's creation. In some Volga cities, to the south-east, conflicts were bloody. But generally the strife was of short duration and low intensity (54:*362,370*).

By the beginning of 1918, urban Russia was under rule by soviets. Unbridled optimism was the Bolshevik mood. All doubts were forgotten. The mainly non-Russian populations of the Ukraine and the Transcaucasus still yearned after autonomy from Petrograd's control; town soviets on the periphery of the former Russian empire declaring allegiance to Sovnarkom, as at Baku in Azerbaidzhan, were rarities (122:*226–7*). Closer to home, in Russia, the peasantry's attitude to Lenin's government was not yet clear. But the Bolshevik party felt no cause for depression. Problems existed only to be solved, or so it seemed at the time. Party activists were channelled into posts in the soviets and other state agencies. A neglect of party life was the consequence, but this was considered acceptable on the grounds that the transfer of personnel aided the implementation of Bolshevik policies. Institutions proliferated. The party leadership not only took over surviving organs of government but also, since these often proved inadequate to their tasks, set up several new ones. The scope for local initiative was broad, and local political pride expanded. The transfer of authority to the soviets in Saratov induced the hyperbolic announcement: 'Our commune is the beginning of the world-wide commune. We, as the leaders, assume full responsibility and fear nothing' (80:*57*). This attitude evoked no resentment in Petrograd. Central intervention in the provinces was restricted; Y. M. Sverdlov, the principal organiser for the party, reiterated that the government's decrees were meant only to provide general guidance and that it was up to the localities to get on with their own revolution (112:*61*). 'Mass practical work' was Lenin's demand. The release of the people's creative potentiality was as great a priority for Sovnarkom as administrative direction from on high.

(ii) Economic and diplomatic prostration: 1917–18

This enthusiasm, however, was counterpointed by the party's underestimation of Russia's economic and foreign-policy emergency. The sceptics in the Central Committee, such as L. B. Kamenev and G. E. Zinoviev, had little following; even Lenin, whose statements before the October Revolution were not devoid of equivocations and silences about the political prospect (110:*12–15*), sustained an ultra-sanguine viewpoint for some weeks. And yet catastrophe impended.

Gaunt statistics delineate the story. In 1917, large and medium-sized factories produced only two-thirds of the output registered for the year before the First World War. Production in such enterprises in 1918 tumbled to a mere third. The industrial economy was being battered to its knees by clusters of blows from the transport breakdowns, from inadequate supplies of raw materials, from the capital investment shortage and from unchecked inflation. In the first ten months of the Soviet regime 38 per cent of the country's large factories had to close (41:*34*). The agrarian sector fared better. The autumn harvest of 1917 was down only 13 per cent on the annual average for 1909–13. But the beginnings of trouble were discernible. The country as a whole was left with a deficit of 13.3 million tons of grain to meet what had been regarded as normal standards of consumption; even southern Russia and the Ukraine had no surplus to 'export' to other regions, and the Volga area (which usually produced more than it needed to feed its own population) reported a shortfall (135:*7,15–16*). The difficulties in the two main sectors of the national economy were aggravated by a third difficulty: in the relations between the two sectors. The contraction in industry made it hard to acquire even half-satisfactory food supplies for the towns because there were too few industrial goods to dispatch to the countryside in exchange.

Quickly the Bolsheviks, like the Provisional Government before them, attracted all the blame for the situation. But there were positive aspects in Sovnarkom's measures. Nationalisation and workers' control prevented many firms from being liquidated by their owners, and profiteering rackets ceased. The authorities also at least did their utmost to convey such manufactured products as did exist to the countryside. Yet the adverse effects of policy weighed heavily in the scales. The party's ultimate goal was the extirpation of capitalism. To put it gently, this did not foster an atmosphere of business confidence. Lenin did not intend to make an instant introduction of socialism throughout the economy; but he was not the entire party, and his less restrained colleagues spoke menacingly about the immediate fate of entre-preneurship (41:*31*). Even the eagerness to end the war made for problems. The government stopped financing armaments production; but the war-orientated factories, which consti-tuted the majority, could not switch to civilian work in short order. Disruption resulted (22:*36,38*).

The young Soviet republic's foreign relations were mean-while crashing into trouble. Trotski as People's Commissar of External Affairs assumed that his task would be to publish the ex-tsar's secret treaties and retire to await the inevitable global conflagration. But the fuse smouldered damply in the winter of 1917–18. Riots, strikes and mutinies were held at governable levels by the Central Powers. German diplomats demanded that Sovnarkom should cede sovereignty over the west of the former Russian empire. At the start, Trotski's scheme of dragging out the negotiations worked well. But in January 1918 the Germans delivered their ultimatum. For most Bolsheviks, both at the centre and in the localities, this left no alternative but to wage 'revolutionary war'. Lenin judged differently. Not to sign a separate peace with Germany and Austria-Hungary appeared to him like the politics of the kindergarten. In February, as the scale of the domestic economic plight and of German military superiority became manifest, others in the party reached the same conclusion. The Bolshevik proponents of a continued war were called the Left Communists. Led by N. I. Bukharin, they found support waning. The Seventh Party Congress in March 1918 sanc-tioned the signing of 'the obscene peace'. The treaty of Brest-Litovsk compelled the Soviet government to abjure claims to the Ukraine, Belorussia and the Baltic region. This involved the loss of two-fifths of the country's industrial resources. It dashed hopes of economic reconstruction and political stabilisation through the emergence of friendly nearby states; and it spelled doom for thoughts of a smooth resolution of the food-supplies difficulty: the cession of the Ukraine meant that grain would have to be procured from regions which could not even feed their own inhabitants (135:*14–16*).

(iii) Social reforms and mass participation

Yet the party was not punished politically for its failures of prediction. Any social revolution, however imposing its ruling elite may be, needs the favour of broad layers of the population. This was obtained in Russia in 1917–18. Sovnarkom's social reforms enjoyed support among workers, peasants and soldiers. Indeed an ethos of self-liberation and civic participation was strongly in evidence. The party did not yet direct all public affairs. On the contrary, most changes at the base of the economy and society were undertaken independently of governmental decrees. Mass politics were no myth. Moreover, the connection between the party and sections of the urban working class was unbroken. Workingmen and women in late 1917 were reportedly 60 per cent of the membership, and their presence ensured for the moment that the aspirations of 'the masses' were being taken seriously.

Workers in Petrograd and in many other places ejected their old managers; many interpreted 'workers' control', much to Lenin's chagrin, as a means of enabling their elected factory committees to go beyond supervising the managerial offices and to take them over completely (117:*228*). The Left Communists in the Bolshevik party, which changed its title to the Russian Communist Party in March 1918, were delighted by this initiative. They were equally pleased by demands from below for a more far-reaching policy of nationalisation. Lenin's Sovnarkom had opted to place only the 'commanding heights' of industry in the hands of the state; and the process was supposed to last many months. In addition, medium-sized and small factories were exempted from governmental takeover. Yet many labour forces refused to accept this restraint and 'nationalised' their firms without consulting the metropolitan authorities (21:*99*). Such introductions of workers' control and state ownership reflected a popular feeling that a new society, free from oppression and exploitation, was being built. They were also a continuation of working-class defensive strategy to impede shutdowns. Thus utopianism and practical prudence were entwined. And thousands of workers, applying their confidence to politics outside the factory gates, volunteered for service in state institutions. Their own mass organisations, like the trade unions, still required their participation; and local and central economic agencies, too, welcomed working-class personnel in order to control officials from the regimes of Nikolai II and the Provisional Government (40:*282–5*). Bolshevik theory had always extolled the urban proletariat as the vanguard of socialist revolution. But numerous workers required little prompting to engage in public affairs, and to ignore this leads to distorted pictures of the October Revolution.

Even so, the auguries for disappointment appeared simultaneously. The general economic situation led to massive unemployment. The average number of gainfully employed factory workers in 1917 fell by 23 per cent in the following year (96:*9*). The most jobs were lost by unskilled labourers; the ties of these with the land tended to be stronger, and factory committees exhorted them to return to their villages to fill their stomachs. But the privilege of staying in the towns, even with a job, was no sinecure. Starvation had become a realistic fear. In Petrograd, it was necessary to drop the official bread ration to a few ounces per day in February.

It is no wonder that workers began to put the interests of their particular enterprise before state interests as interpreted by Sovnarkom. Disruptive localism was increasingly the subject of complaint by the government. The peasantry's self-preoccupation caused equal concern. Peasants wanted and got their own revolution. Both the land decree of October and the Basic Law, promulgated four months later, essentially sanctioned this; such clauses as contradicted the peasantry's desires, like the ban on breaking up the large capitalist estates, were locally ignored (54:*395,400–1*). Nearly 50,000 'agitators' sped out from the towns before midsummer 1918 (11:*4*). Their impact was probably small. Rural self-rule held. This was accompanied by a further strengthening of the communes.

Regional differences persisted, but a pattern was widely clear. By 1920 only 4 per cent of peasant households in 39 provinces of European Russia existed outside the communal structure (3:*209*). Confiscations of non-peasant land continued. In Russia's central agricultural region, peasants gained direct control over an area about a quarter larger than they had owned before; and in the Ukraine it was around three-quarters (3:*181–2*). Yet few households became instantly rich. Nearly all families held so little land that even a proportionate increase of that order would not save them from poverty. Land hunger did not vanish. Furthermore, most of the noble-owned fields seized by the peasantry in 1917–18 had anyway been rented and farmed by peasants for years. Thus the actual area under their cultivation expanded only slightly. Nevertheless the advantages accruing as a result of the Revolution were not trivial. A little land was better than no extra land. Payments to landlords ceased. Mortage debts were annulled. And it was satisfying for peasants to look out upon a landscape from which it seemed that oppressive agents of government had been permanently removed.

Rural commercial intransigence hardened. Peasant households were alarmed by the rising inflation and by the dearth of industrial products on sale. The state still had responsibilities for feeding soldiers and workers; and a system of completely free trade would probably have lowered the amount of wheat procured by Sovnarkom. A further cut-back in rations would have resulted. A few soviets temporarily suspended the grain monopoly (85:*56*). Elsewhere illegal bartering was on the increase. Possibly Sovnarkom would have been more prudent to requisition a bare minimum of supplies and allow the peasantry to sell the remainder privately. After all, the size of the army and the working class was diminishing fast in the winter of 1917–18. But an ideological factor made the suggestion unfeasible. The Bolsheviks found it repugnant to show greater indulgence to private enterprise than Kerenski's government, including the Socialist-Revolutionary Chernov, had done. The alternative was to use force alone. Authorities from some towns adopted this option in early 1918, and impounding of grain followed. Clashes with the local peasantry occurred (54:*431*).

57

(iv) Repression

The divergence in the requirements of workers and peasants was a blow for a party with a programme based upon the premise that these two classes should stay in alliance. On the other hand, the Bolsheviks had always regarded the peasantry as the less reliable of the two social groups; and some provincial party leaders were annoyed that a scheme to make peasants stop farming for profit and pool their land and labour in socialist collectives had not been put in hand (130:*95–6*). The conflicts in the countryside within months of October 1917 reinforced the party's suspicions about the peasantry. The Bolshevik leadership was undoubtedly a victim of circumstances, but it was also a victimiser. The trouble in the villages came in succession to acts of political intolerance in the towns. Bolshevik theory had always been an unstable amalgam of notions of liberation from below and notions of direction from above. Lenin and Trotski opposed proposals for Mensheviks and Socialist Revolutionaries to join Sovnarkom because of their participation in Kerenski's ministry. Several Bolshevik Central Committee members and People's Commissars were aghast at this. It is a sign of the patchiness of the party leadership's thinking that an insurrection had been carried through without prior discussion as to who was to belong to the new administration. Lenin now got his way. His dissenting colleagues resigned; and the rupture of negotiations with the Mensheviks and Socialist Revolutionaries began the affront to those countless workers who had backed the seizure of power on the assumption that a regime uniting all socialist parties would be formed (61:*266,335*;74:*326–7*).

And yet it also has to be understood that the October Revolution itself had briskly reduced the already meagre space for compromise. Few Mensheviks and fewer Socialist Revolutionaries would join a government which included Lenin. Calls for the forcible removal of the Bolsheviks were commonplace. The Mensheviks were the only party in opposition to refrain from such a summons, and even they contained groups advocating armed struggle with Sovnarkom. Meanwhile the forces of the far political right were reassembling.

58

General Alekseev gathered a Volunteer Army in southern Russia. Not a few Kadets wished him well; some were even to prove willing to welcome German occupation. The Bolshevik Central Committee was not absolutely averse to the proposal of a coalition. It asked the Left Socialist Revolutionaries, who had broken away from the Party of Socialist Revolutionaries in late summer, to join Sovnarkom in October. The first invitation was rejected. But eventually, in November, the Left Socialist Revolutionaries became the junior partners in the Soviet government.

All such allowances notwithstanding, the Bolshevik central leaders contributed decisively to the aggravation of intolerance and violence. Before October, Lenin had often mitigated his vocabulary of dictatorship and civil war (110:*14*). Trotski and others had been less temperate. Soon after October, immoderacy became normal. Arrests of Kadets and closures of their newspapers took place. The creation of an Extraordinary Commission (or *Cheka*) in December signalled the crossing of a fateful threshold. The intention was to eradicate counter-revolution and sabotage; but the Commission was relieved of the need to follow judicial procedures in collecting evidence and carrying out sentence. Then, on 5 January 1918, came the first session of the Constituent Assembly. The Bolsheviks had done well electorally in the towns: most workers who voted appear to have favoured them. But their party received only 21 per cent of all votes. The Socialist Revolutionaries, with their huge rural support, did massively better with 38 per cent (and this did not even include the backing for their sister parties in non-Russian regions) (94:*30*). It was the first and last freely-contested election in the country's history. Sovnarkom flatly refused to abide by the result. The Constituent Assembly was forcibly dispersed, and scores of persons were shot in street demonstrations. The urban working class had never been monolithically pro-Bolshevik. The economic conditions and the spectacle of violence strengthened dissent. In spring 1918, the Bolsheviks were defeated in some town soviet elections in central Russia (9:*4*). Again the polls were ruled invalid. And in Petrograd, where Bolshevik authorities kept a tighter grip upon the City Soviet, thousands of hostile workers established their own

59

Assembly of Plenipotentiaries. Force was used to crush it (25:*17*).

These measures revealed the Bolshevik party's ruthlessness; but they were equally an index of its fragile political position. The government's existence was threatened. Yet it survived not just because its coercive agencies were fierce but also because popular approval of Sovnarkom's early economic decrees remained. The promotion of factory labourers into public office, in addition, strengthened the Soviet state internally; and the party itself could still boast that most of its rank-and-file members were of working-class origin. The chances of overthrowing the Bolsheviks were weaker than they seemed. Hunger, unemployment and the flight from the towns cut back the potential for organised resistance. The soviets had been proud bases of independent social activity in 1917. But they required many more years of exceptionally favourable circumstances if they were going to maintain their integrity against the Bolshevik resolve to bend them permanently to the party's will. Disunity and low morale among the anti-Bolsheviks made Lenin's task easier still.

(v) Civil War: 1917–21

A civil war exploded. Seizures of power striking at the roots of property laws, like the October Revolution, are inherently likely to spark off armed struggle. In China in 1949 and Cuba in 1959 the old regime's demolition was the culmination of the fighting. In Russia, the events of October signalled the first approaches to protracted regular warfare. Soviet forces were sent into the Ukraine in December 1917. Their success was short-lived. To the north, the German military menace induced the transfer of the capital from Petrograd to Moscow in February 1918, and the Brest-Litovsk treaty necessitated a Soviet withdrawal from the Ukraine. In May, a further contraction of territory occurred. A legion of Czechoslovak former prisoners-of-war revolted against Sovnarkom. They swept aside the Bolshevik-led soviets from Siberia through to the river Volga. For months, Nikolai II and his family had been held in detention in the Urals. The Soviet authorities were afraid lest the Czechoslovak legion might liberate them, and had them all executed. The retreat before the Czechoslovaks continued. Reaching Samara, the legion welcomed the formation of a government of Socialist-Revolutionary members of the Constituent Assembly; and yet another administration, representing several anti-Bolshevik parties, was set up in Omsk in Siberia. Meanwhile the Left Socialist Revolutionaries, infuriated by Brest-Litovsk and by grain requisitioning, left the Sovnarkom coalition. The Soviet government had been organising a Workers' and Peasants' Red Army since February. These troops were rushed down to retake the Volga towns. Even so, the troubles of the Bolsheviks were about to become greater. The Volunteer Army, commanded by General A. I. Denikin upon the death of Alekseev, was on the move in the south. In the autumn, Admiral Kolchak assembled another contingent of reactionary imperial officers in Siberia. These two White armies, as they were called to distinguish them from the 'Reds', had little intention of restoring the Constituent Assembly. In fact the first action of the putatively amphibian Kolchak's followers in November was to crush the Omsk government backed by the Socialist-Revolutionaries.

The descent into all-out civil war strengthened the moves made since early 1918 to overhaul the Soviet state machine. Centralism, discipline and demarcation had begun to be introduced in a piecemeal fashion. Soviets and trade unions had undergone a measure of internal reconstruction; it had been recognised that the revolutionary order of October 1917 had produced much disorderliness. Politics, too, had had a disruptive impact. The Brest-Litovsk controversy had come close to tearing both the government and the Bolshevik party asunder. From midsummer 1918, with the drastic worsening of the situation at the front line, the case for administrative reform became irrefutable. Hierarchical authority was exerted in every public institution. The party was transformed. The Bolsheviks, long-time theorists of organisational centralism, were practising what they had preached; and, moreover, power at the party's apex was devolved from the Central Committee to two inner subcommittees in January 1919. The Politburo decided grand strategy and high policy, the Orgburo oversaw internal administration. The passage of authority to fewer officials occurred also in local party bodies. The party's functions were greatly expanded. In effect, it became the supreme agency of state. In 1918 there had been confusion between the duties of Sovnarkom and the Central Committee. The Politburo's ascendancy was a watershed (109:*86–7*).

These arrangements were not quite as neat in reality as on paper. The party lost personnel to the Red Army, and its supervisory capacity was therefore limited at times (7:*197–8*). Both the army and the Cheka retained much independence in their day-to-day operations. The Politburo had to struggle to keep control. But results, not formal means, were its concern. Its own internal procedures were flexible. Lenin on occasion issued instructions after a telephone conversation with his Politburo colleagues but without a proper meeting (and he might often add his signature as Sovnarkom chairman to lend extra strength to a document). Wartime, in the belief of Bolsheviks, necessitated exceptional measures. Violations of even Soviet legislation were condoned so long as they aided the war effort. The style of work throughout the state was frenetic. It was also intimidating. Trotski, as People's Commissar for Military Affairs, employed thousands of officers from the imperial armed forces to staff his Red Army. To each of them he attached a 'political commissar' to ensure loyalty, and hostages from their families were also taken. Not that the Soviet state was without its attractiveness to many non-socialists. Pre-war officials, both civil and military, had chances of rapid promotion. The party also maintained its efforts to obtain the sympathy of the non-Russian nationalities. Russian chauvinism was disowned. But the principle of national self-determination was honoured no longer. The Red Army was charged with the task of reconquering; it was not asked to hold plebiscites about state frontiers. Not that internationalist ideals had faded entirely. Links were sought with far-left political groups abroad; and in March 1919 the founding Congress of the Communist International (or Komintern), which was to unify and direct communist parties around the globe, was held in Moscow.

'Everything for the front' was the slogan. The battles against the White armies began again in spring 1919. By autumn, both were defeated. Kolchak's forces had retreated deep into Siberia by midsummer. Their plight left the Red Army free to roll back Denikin's two-pronged attack along the Volga and through the Ukraine. A third White army under General Yudenich moved out from Estonia on Petrograd in October. Never a serious military threat, it was easily crushed. Kolchak was caught and executed in February 1920. Denikin handed over his command to General P. N. Wrangel, but this last White army's breakout from the Crimean peninsula was short-lived. By autumn 1920 the civil war's outcome was put beyond doubt.

This remarkable victory, according to Soviet spokesmen then and now, was achieved to a large extent through the government's alteration of economic policies. Changes had begun in early 1918, and were strengthened when the fighting intensified. Sovnarkom's objections to accelerated industrial nationalisation lapsed. Nearly all large factories were state-owned by January 1919, and virtually all medium-sized ones by the end of the same year. These confiscations made valuable stocks publicly available (41:*46*). Universal labour obligations were made law. Strict discipline was demanded in factories, and the urban propertied classes were compelled to toil as snow-clearers and defence-works diggers. Town-made products were to be dispatched mainly to the Red Army (41:*38*). Food distribution was given the same priority. Forcible requisitioning of grain, which had been practised spasmodically in early 1918, was turned into a system. Collaboration was sought from the less well-off peasants. In May 1918 the government summoned each village to establish a 'committee of the rural poor' to identify the richer families hoarding a food surplus. In February 1919, a step further was taken. Instead of sending out detachments to discover hoards, the authorities in Moscow assigned a delivery quota to each province which had to be met even where the local peasants in fact had nothing to spare if they were to feed themselves and conserve enough seed for sowing (16:*170–1*).

Such measures were practical reactions to circumstances. But there was equally an ideological element. All politicians operate with a bundle of prior judgements and inclinations. Even a notorious manœuvrer like Lloyd George had his fixed opinions. Bolshevik ideas, moreover, had exceptional durability. Fired in the kiln of the party's powerlessness and persecution before 1917, they retained their robustness subsequently. The desire for a de-privatised, moneyless, centrally-controlled economy was strongly felt. Even Lenin, who had proposed a more cautious pace of change in industry and agriculture in the October Revolution, caught the excitement.

And yet the economics of 'War Communism', as the period came to be dubbed, were not especially successful. Factory output in 1920 was a seventh of the total in 1913, and governmental procurement of food was lower than under the Provisional Government (41:*34*). The Whites were at no disadvantage in this respect. Kolchak and Denikin received military supplies from Britain and France; and their forces started from regions rich in grain. But otherwise the Reds were more fortunate. Victory for the Allies in the First World War in November 1918 at a stroke dispelled the possibility of German interference. And the British and French contingents which disembarked in Archangel and Odessa respectively saw next to no action. The Allies suspended their intervention at the end of 1919. In addition, Kolchak and Denikin made trouble for themselves by talking about their vision of 'Russia one and indivisible'. This caused offence and fear among non-Russians. In particular, the anti-semitic mayhem of White officers secured the Jewish population on the Bolshevik side. Latvians, too, supplied highly effective units to the Reds. Even a detachment of Cossacks, traditionally a very conservative group, was willing to form a Red Cavalry. The use of horses in the roadless countryside was important. The mode of fighting was highly mobile; the cross-trench techniques of the First World War were redundant. The Whites were constantly hampered by the geography of the railways. The Bolsheviks never lost Moscow and Petrograd. They held the two centres whence the country's communications and transport arteries extended. This logistical superiority was crucial. Neither side had a monopoly of strategical error. But the Red Army's chances of recuperation were greater, and there was no White leader who had quite the directing verve of Bolsheviks like Lenin, Trotski and Stalin.

Moreover, the Politburo had greater appeal in politics in general. Neither Kolchak nor Denikin publically advocated the seizure of gentry land back from the peasantry. But their subordinates were reactionaries. Peasant 'ringleaders' were hanged, and the estates went back to the old landowners in areas under White occupation. Execution awaited Bolshevik activists in the towns. The Socialist Revolutionaries, who recognised the imprudence of any such total assault upon the popular gains of 1917, were swept aside (and many of them, compelled to choose between Reds and Whites, joined Trotski's army). Kadets filled many posts in the White civil administration. Yet they too met with suspicion from the military commanders; and few Kadet functionaries had the nerve to restrain the Whites from their outrages upon the local populace. The Bolshevik party's programme put it in good stead by comparison. The word went forth in *Pravda*, by 'agit-trains' and on the lips of soldiers and activists: a Red victory in the civil war was the sole guarantee that the former ruling and propertied groups would not resume their power.

(vi) Opposition to Bolshevism

Nevertheless the margin of popularity enjoyed by the Bolsheviks could have been much wider. The military strife had been a close-run thing, and the Reds would have shortened the odds against themselves if they had abandoned some policies sooner. The Cheka ran amok. Atrocities were committed against the urban middle class; and several thousand workers and peasants also ended up in prison, sometimes for no more heinous offence than trading in grain in order to remain alive (69:*178*). Agrarian measures discredited the party further. The committees of the village poor, set up in mid 1918, were abolished before the year was out because most peasant households resented them. Even so, pressure on the peasants was maintained. In the Ukraine, efforts were made to force them into collective farms (130:*95–6*). The Politburo overruled such schemes. But its members firmly persisted with grain requisitioning. By 1920 they treated it as permanent policy. This was inviting trouble. In the same year, party bodies pushed their luck in the towns as well. Factory discipline was taken to the length of transferring military conscripts to 'labour armies' instead of de-mobilising them. Nor had the ambition to spread the revolution abroad been buried. The Polish army under Pilsudski seized Kiev in spring 1920. The Reds counter-attacked. A rapid campaign brought them within striking range of Warsaw.

Violent upheavals were not unique to the former Russian empire after the First World War. In January 1919, the German Spartakists briefly sustained an uprising in Berlin. In March 1919, soviet republics were proclaimed in Bavaria and Hungary; and, in 1920, the workers' council movement in northern Italy came near to producing national revolution. And yet the scale and duration of carnage was greatest of all in Russia, and only the fighting in Hungary rivalled it in brutality. The sufferings were enormous. The country's population declined absolutely by 7 million from 1918 to 1923, with deaths from disease outnumbering deaths in battle (72:*30–1*). Killings were plentiful behind the front lines. The combatant forces and their leaderships, both civil and military, bore a grievous responsibility for the dimensions of the bloodshed, but they themselves were also deeply affected by their involvement in the process. Bolshevism in particular registered the impact. The contest between mass persuasion and massive coercion, in the party's ideas, moved ever more decisively in favour of violence. Harsh abstractions about dictatorship and civil war had lain in the tissue of Bolshevik thought for years. The strife after the October Revolution force-fed their gross development.

An army-style control over society increased after 1918. But obedience was a vast distance from perfection (as even straightforwardly military governments, such as Pinochet's in Chile from 1974, usually discover). The regulation of the industrial labour market proved impossible. An acute shortage of workers, especially those with skills, prevailed (41:*87*). Nor could the state ensure maintained agricultural acreages. The area sown to grain in 1921 was down at least 16 per cent on 1913, and in all probability down a lot further still (3:*226*; 90:*243*). Food-supply laws were flouted. Approximately half of

66

what was eaten in the towns came through blackmarketeering 'sack-men' who bought up stores in the countryside (134:*599*). In the Red Army there were grave problems of discipline. In 1919 the number of classified deserters, which included many men who had simply not answered their call-up papers, reached a million; this was not far short of the total of those actually serving at the battlefronts (60:*396,463*). Resistance to the Soviet authorities took increasingly active forms. Factory strikes broke out in Moscow and Petrograd in the civil war. The countryside was in turmoil. Official spokesmen cautiously admitted that 344 peasant revolts erupted by mid-1919 (69:*329*). In 1920, overt opposition intensified. A rural rebellion gripped Tambov province from end to end. The Ukraine and western Siberia were bases for 'Green' guerrillas who hated the Whites and Reds equally. The strike movement in the cities was in crescendo. The Kronstadt naval garrison was on the brink of mutiny by February 1921. Peasant insurgents, striking workers and sailor mutineers did not co-ordinate their activity. But their demands were alike. They called for the abolition of grain sequestrations, for a boosting of food supplies, for the reintroduction of free competition among the political parties.

The ring of hostile forces tightened. In August 1920, the Polish army unexpectedly vanquished the Reds at the battle of the Vistula and peace negotiations ensued. At home, the party was relied upon to shore up the regime. But this too was problematic. Wartime centralisation had lessened but not eliminated friction between local and central Bolshevik bodies. Disputes now gathered in disruptiveness. In addition, more workers left the party's ranks in protest against War Communism; less than two-fifths of rank-and-filers were of working-class origin by 1920 (112:*148*).

(vii) The NEP and economic recovery: 1921–27

In February 1921 the Politburo resolved upon a major reform. This became known as the New Economic Policy (or NEP). Grain requisitioning was abolished. It was replaced by a graduated tax in kind, and the target set for collection was less

67

than 4 million tons of cereal whereas nearly 7 million had been sought in 1920. Peasants could trade the remainder of their grain legally. The Tenth Party Congress approved the turn-about in March 1921; it also sent out delegates to crush the Kronstadt mutiny. All political opposition was to be smashed. Socialist-Revolutionary leaders were put on show trial in 1922 and sentenced to lengthy terms of imprisonment. The Tenth Congress also banned factions inside the Bolshevik party. The Democratic Centralists had urged the curtailing of the Polit-buro's authority; the Workers' Opposition wanted working people to have greater control over economic decisions. Both factions were suppressed. This rigidification was thought necessary if economic retreats were to be accomplished with-out political destabilisation. Private enterprise returned to industry in 1921. Small factories had traditionally supplied many goods bought by peasants, and, in order to create conditions which would attract rural households into market-ing their grain surplus in the towns, a host of such firms were leased back to their former owners by the state. By 1923 only 2 per cent of workers in small-scale industry were governmental employees (42:*204*). Redoubled efforts were made to restore commerce with foreign nations. On the other hand, there were limits to compromise under the terms of the New Economic Policy. Large factories, the banks and foreign trade remained in the government's hands. Central industrial planning, too, remained an objective.

Yet politics continued to be turbulent. As the more recent experience of Kenya and other African states suggests, the creation of a one-party state concentrates and can even aggravate dissent in the single official party. And there were plenty of controversial issues from 1921. The NEP itself was a gigantic gamble. The shrinking of the urban population and demobilisation had lowered the government's food-supplies requirements; but the tax-collection level set in 1921 was below even these more modest needs. Workers were kept on rations. Other sections of the populace of the towns had this provision withdrawn (133:*346*). Worse still, the harvest of 1921 was poor. Hundreds of thousands of peasants starved to death in the Volga region. Diplomatic reverses added to the distress. The French and British delegations at an international conference in Genoa in 1922 spurned the Soviet request for reacceptance into the world trading community; only the Germans, from among the great powers, would initially co-operate. In addition, domestic pricing policy was mishandled. Peasants by 1923 were being asked to pay three times as much, in real value, for urban products as in 1913. They stopped trading their grain in reaction.

Nevertheless the NEP was retained as a treatment. The doses were adjusted to deal with each set-back, and a general economic recuperation occurred; and this achievement, no less than the coercion used to administer the medicine, helps to explain the policy's widespread acceptance. Agriculture and industry benefited. Grain production in 1926 was roughly the same as the annual average between 1909 and 1913. Livestock husbandry achieved greater than pre-war productivity. The movement towards a more diversified and intensive agriculture, begun in the imperial period, was resumed. In 1913, 90 per cent of the sown area was given to cereal cultivation; by 1928, only 82 per cent was needed (137:*4*). Sugar-beet, potatoes and cotton made much progress. Technical sophistication grew. There were more horse-drawn machines in annual supply in the second half of the twenties than before the First World War (18:*8*); and multi-field crop rotation was being applied in 17 per cent of sowings in the Russian Socialist Federal Soviet Republic in 1927 as compared with 1.5 per cent for the same area in 1916 (15:*278*). Such figures give the lie to notions that the agrarian sector, having forfeited the benefits of capitalist estate management, slid into stagnancy. The NEP made progress at its own moderate pace. In the industrial sector, too, there occurred a lively restoration. Private small-scale and handicrafts output rose to about the same level in the tax year 1926–7 as in 1913. And in the large-scale factories, where state ownership predominated, the prophets of doom were again disproved. Estimates differ. Some put industrial production in 1926–7 in all types of enterprise only slightly lower than in 1913; others suggest that it was up to 6 per cent higher (45:*186–7*;137:*3*). Nor did the NEP entail a withdrawal of investment in industry (10:*425*). Engineering capacity outstripped that of the pre-war period, and the proportion of output in industry in general which was reinvested in production was no lower than under Nikolai II (137:*6*).

The possibility of sustaining an annual growth rate in factory activity of 6 per cent (137:*6*) was no mean performance for a socialist state surrounded on all sides by hostile capitalist powers. 'Socialism In One Country' was becoming the regime's rallying cry; but economic isolation in reality was neither without advantages nor quite complete. The unilateral cancellation of milliards of roubles of governmental debts in 1917 meant that Russia never had to shoulder the burdens imposed on Germany through the reparations demanded by the treaty of Versailles in 1919. The United Kingdom, moreover, restored trading links with the Soviet republic in 1924. Trade with the world increased over the 1920s. The export of oil was more than double the volume registered before the First World War (10:*971*); and the government, using this receipt of foreign currency as well as attracting concessionnaires in industry, strove to renovate the country's technological base. In some key industries, such as oil extraction, the effort was crowned with success (123:*43–4*). Purchases abroad were also crucial. Two-fifths of the machinery and other capital equipment bought in 1926–7 were imported (10:*413,971*).

(viii) The recuperation of society

Debates on economic strategy were common to European politics after the World War. They were especially intensive and public in Russia. The goal of a mature industrial society was shared by all party and nearly all government officials (whereas uncountable numbers of bureaucrats and landlords had found industrialism abhorrent under the old regime). This aided the economy's recovery. In addition, labour relations became more tranquil than at any time earlier in the century. At the end of the civil war, Trotski had urged the outlawing of strikes. In fact, the working-class gains of the October Revolution were never so drastically cut back. Strikes did occur. But they were few; the most troublesome year was 1927, when 396 stoppages took place: only 20,100 workers were involved (20:*144*). The party emphasised conciliation.

Lip-service was offered to the need to remove restrictive work practices so as to raise productivity; time-and-motion specialists toured enterprises. But their recommendations were seldom enforced. Trade union central leaderships were exclusively Bolshevik and did not sanction strikes in state-owned concerns, but nonetheless their bargaining activity was not wholly perfunctory. The working class, furthermore, welcomed the increase in job vacancies under the NEP. In 1920 there had been only 1.2 million labourers employed in the large factories; by 1926–7 the figure had risen to 2.8 million (10:*955*). Men who had moved to the villages or served in the Red Army in the civil war returned to resume their old trades. Women, after being welcomed into the factories in wartime, tended to get pushed out. In 1921, the wages were probably only a third of what they had been in 1913 in real terms (143:*390*). But conditions improved. By the tax year 1927–8 the tsarist wage level had been reattained, and may even have been surpassed by 24 per cent (10:*606*). For some of the unemployed, too, there was a degree of amelioration: the state for the first time in Russia provided financial relief.

This betterment helps to explain the regime's survival. Yet forces for social instability persisted. The increase in factory jobs did not eradicate mass unemployment. In 1927 over a million workers were registered as unemployed. Hiring and firing arrangements, even in state factories, could still be peremptory (10:*468–9*). Some observers predicted that the party would shortly feel compelled to institute more far-reaching reforms. Small-time traders, known as 'nepmen', strove to make the commercial big time. Shops selling luxury products reopened on Petrograd's Nevski Prospekt; several novels which contained criticisms of the Soviet order, albeit restrictedly and often indirectly, were passed by the censorship and became best-sellers.

And so the party's expectation of an uninterrupted, triumphal march to socialism was brusquely shaken. Most workers were indifferent to its ideas; it galled party propagandists that Charlie Chaplin films outstripped those of the Soviet *avant-guarde* political cinema in popularity (127:*65*). The peasantry, moreover, lived almost unaffected by the mass media. The official press did not transform rural opinion, and agronomists and surveyors remained a rare sight in most villages. Land communes under the NEP regulated the lives of nine-tenths of European Russia's rural households. Atheistic communism made little impact upon the peasantry's Christian faith (or upon Islam in the southern and eastern reaches of the republic) (6:*77*). Sexual mores seem to have altered little, and this was true also of townspeople (33:*121*). Not that change was quite absent. Younger peasants, gaining confidence through their experiences either in the Revolution or in the Red Army, stood up to their elders more stoutly (114:*176*). But this did not lead to a break with many economic customs in the countryside. In 1917–18, to be sure, there had been a levelling of conditions among households; the proportions of the peasantry classifiable respectively as rich and poor were reduced. Even so, social differentiation quickly resumed its course. The Bolsheviks initially strove to impede such a development by forbidding the leasing of land and the hiring of labour. The prohibitions were unenforcible. The government recognised this by a series of piecemeal reforms in the 1920s. Inequalities in circumstances returned. By the tax year 1927–8, they were such that 56 per cent of the net sales of grain in European Russia were made by no more than 11 per cent of households (18:*25–7*).

So were the conditions of the peasantry very different from what had prevailed under Nikolai II? The question awaits systematic investigation, but an important piece of the evidence is that more grain stayed with the peasants in the NEP period; the percentage of the harvest leaving the countryside fell from twenty to fifteen, and quite possibly even lower to less than ten, between 1913 and 1926–7 (18:*17*;10:*941*). More peasants, and more of their livestock, ate more and better. Hardly any 'disturbances' are reported as having occurred in the countryside in the mid 1920s.

(ix) The party and the political system

Yet the NEP was no paradise for the peasantry. The real cost of industrial goods in the villages remained higher under the NEP than before the First World War. The policy involved a balance between the respective demands of many social groups, and those of workers, peasants and administrators were handled with particular care by the authorities. Life in the state bureaucracy settled down after the convulsions of 1917–20; pay and conditions for civil servants improved. The power of government was imposed cautiously but firmly after 1921. The Politburo's confidence stemmed in no small measure from the fact that years of repression and warfare had cast down all the institutional impediments to its dominance. And the Bolshevik leadership, which had always laid greater store by guiding than by reflecting social opinion, wanted no threat to this status quo. Political violence in fact diminished after the civil war. Outright counter-revolution had been exported: between 1 and 3 million people had emigrated in the years of turmoil, and these came mainly from the middle and upper classes (89:*87*). A menace remained on the political left. A couple of small, anti-Bolshevik communist parties were formed. But they were quickly broken up by a Cheka which was not overexerted in the 1920s. The Red Army was trimmed in size. The country was not attacked from abroad; and internal armed strife, apart from a Georgian revolt in 1924 and Moslem guerrilla warfare in central Asia, gave little bother. Of course, the authorities left nothing to chance. The Solovki island prison awaited recalcitrant active opposition. Lenin's Russia in the years of the NEP still outmatched Nikolai II's in political unfreedom. The Bolsheviks had an unshakable monopoly of power. Before 1917, the most that the monarchy had achieved was to restrict the brood of parties to a scrawny, ill-lit existence.

The Soviet regime, however, was not just a master butcher; it also refined some skills at political husbandry. The new commercial rights were confirmed. True, local soviet officials sporadically sanctioned police raids on private businesses, but generally the attempt was made to allay the suspicions of peasants, traders and small industrialists. Likewise the persecution of the Orthodox Church, though by no means abandoned, was slackened. It was recognised that both anti-Christian and anti-Islamic violence would merely provoke unrest. The state's authority in general, furthermore, was to be exercised with greater circumspection and predictability. A higher premium than ever was set upon technical expertise. Non-Bolshevik 'specialists' were attracted into Soviet institutions in growing numbers; and Menshevik economists gained particular prominence. The favour of non-Russian nationalities, too, was courted. The Union of Soviet Socialist Republics formally came into being in 1924. Moscow retained direction over all foreign and most domestic policy, but the various territorial units like the Ukrainian Soviet Republic nevertheless gained substantial influence over local institutions of education, health and justice.

Yet there were limits to Bolshevik self-adaptiveness. A single party ruled, and the Politburo still ruled the party. Lenin was not dictator. But his persuasiveness and determination usually won the day; and, no less importantly, he often held the ring between the 'left' and the 'right' inside the Politburo. Outside the party, he retained the chairmanship of Sovnarkom. The complexities of a mixed economy called for detailed decision-making beyond the competence of the small central party apparatus. The significance of Sovnarkom increased accordingly (103:*109*). But Lenin died in 1924. Immediately the Politburo reinforced its grip. Other central party bodies, especially the Orgburo and the Secretariat, had anyway been strengthening their power since the civil war. A disciplined hierarchy of committees in the provinces was an objective shared by the entire Politburo, and the selection of personnel became a crucial matter. Inevitably the post of General Secretary, held by Stalin from 1922, acquired influence. Shortly before his death, Lenin had decided that Stalin was too crude and unscrupulous. But his bid to eject him from the Secretariat came too late. And the central machine's control over the party intensified in the mid-1920s. Peremptory commands became typical. Yet the pattern of obedience was not allowed to petrify into pen-pushing and the quietude of routine. Each local committee secretary had to be hyperactive. He had to show initiative; he was expected to cut through bureaucratic red-tape and flout rules whenever the higher goals of the Politburo were endangered. The NEP's emphasis upon procedural regularity was far from being absolute. Action and achievement were the priority as before (112:*172–3,207*).

The Politburo did not obtain total satisfaction. The ban on factions in the party was not fully enforced. Disputes split the Politburo itself, and the need for adjudication led to a retrieval of some authority by the Central Committee (and by the Central Control Commission, which was established in 1920 to supervise the implementing of policies). Furthermore, Sovnarkom's Commissariats did not accept instructions unquestioningly from the party. Something like pressure groupings emerged in the political system in the 1920s. As in today's USSR and all other countries, governmental functionaries often supplied both advice and information which suited their institution's interest. Bolshevik party members working in Commissariats were no exception. Successive leaders of the Supreme Council of the National Economy exemplified the trend with their arguments in favour of boosting state investment in industry (19:*247*). Inter-institutional alliances based in a particular geographical area flourished informally. Politicians in the Donbass and in the Urals had a habit of proposing measures for the rapid expansion of coal-mining (32:*154*). The Politburo perceived the existence of such lobbying and, by deploying the Workers' and Peasants' Inspectorate to conduct separate enquiries into major issues, it tried to avoid being blatantly misinformed. Financial corruption was also investigated (99:*131,140*). But the most intractable task by far for the Inspectorate was to ensure that the state's normal, everyday administration was properly handled. Russia, especially in its villages, remained in many ways 'under-governed' (83:*132*). The density of the public network of regulation and service was low. Worse still, the offices of government were justifiably notorious for insensitivity, and queues of anxious citizens clutching letters of request or complaint were a persistent feature of the scene.

This in turn aggravated worries about the two-way link between the party and the urban working class. Forged in 1917, it had worn ever thinner. But it did not break. The party developed its talent for persuasion, promotion and manipulation. Thousands of primers with titles such as *The ABC Of Communism* explained the ultimate aims of Bolshevism. Poster art flourished. Lenin, that inveterate irreconcilable, finished by becoming a symbol for national as well as Bolshevik unity.

Peasants travelled to petition him personally as once they had journeyed to the emperor. A cult of Lenin grew up, especially after his death in 1924. State rituals were fostered. Processions and festivals were devised to celebrate occasions in the calendar associated with socialism. The Bolsheviks understood that it was better that workers took to the streets for a holiday than that they were forbidden from massing in public at all and resented the entire political order. Celebration was coupled with organisation. Cultural and sporting societies sprang up with state funding (104:*98,110*). The trade unions had nearly 10 million members by 1927 (10:*545*). To be sure, apathy and hostility remained and even grew. But the effects of the party's drive to keep the working class at least acquiescent in Bolshevik political hegemony cannot be entirely discounted. Campaigns to recruit factory labourers into the party recurred in the 1920s. By 1927, about 55 per cent of the membership claimed working-class backgrounds (101:*116*). The concern remained to promote such newcomers into posts of administration. The Bolsheviks worried frantically about being undermined by a civil service of middle-class origin. The counter-measures were not unimpressive. Surveys in 1926 and 1928 disconfirmed the fear that a majority of Soviet state administrative personnel had held state posts under the monarchy (120:*343*).

(x) Moscow and the world in 1927

And yet from 1927 the NEP itself was in an advanced stage of dissolution. At first sight, this is baffling. The NEP had helped to reset the industrial and agricultural sectors on tracks of economic development, and the chances of further advance were robust. The popular desire for a better standard of living, furthermore, was unabated; and, if the Bolsheviks' economic performance merely matched the tsarist record (which was itself highly commendable), in politics they were more effective in reducing turmoil. The NEP avoided attacks from without the party and government by shunning the excessive inflexibility which had made the absolute monarchy's rule so brittle.

This failed to save it from internal assault. No Bolshevik

leader in 1921 had envisaged the NEP otherwise than as a temporary retreat. Lenin came round, on occasion, to wanting the policy to be maintained for a lengthy period; but he died without divulging a final judgement. Bukharin on the other hand offered a definite analysis. Radically altering strategy, he presented the NEP not as a retreat at all but as the occupation of a ridge from which to undertake the eventual ascent to socialism. Industrialisation and even collective farming could be fostered within its parameters (12:*177*). Such a recasting had critics in the party. In 1923, these formed the Left Opposition under the inspiration of Trotski and E. A. Preobrazhenski. Factional conflict among Bolsheviks surged back. The Left Opposition, disdaining to make favourable comparisons of present and past, contrasted present with wished-for future. For all its vigour, NEP had areas of debility. The metal-extractive enterprises in 1926 produced less than half of the 1913 amount. Armaments output lagged. The technological gap between the USSR and the major capitalist countries widened, particularly in the machine-tools industries. In agriculture, the size of the units of production still gave cause for concern. Kulaks were not 'big farmers' of a type familiar in the West; and in 1927 there were only 24,504 tractors in the Soviet republic (10:*945*). International relations gave rise to juddering trepidation. The British Conservative cabinet broke off trade links in 1927. War scares recurred in the decade. And the Left Opposition, as Bolsheviks, contended that the NEP's success depended upon an increase in affluence of private traders and the better-off peasants. They drew attention to urban unemployment. They complained that in 1927 less than 1 per cent of the USSR's sown area belonged to collective farms (10:*940*).

Such arguments were dismissed by the ascendant party leadership of Zinoviev, Kamenev, Stalin and Bukharin in the mid 1920s. The adhesion of Zinoviev and Kamenev to Trotski's side in 1926, in order to form the United Opposition, made no difference. By 1927 Stalin and Bukharin had defeated them and their followers. Oppositionists either recanted or suffered expulsion from the party and, in some cases, exile. The United Opposition had never been a comprehensively democratic platform. They wanted a Bolshevik party political monopoly as much as other Bolsheviks did; and, though they

77

talked of reintroducing democratic procedures to the party itself, it is open to doubt that their commitment was strong. More open forms of decision, in addition, might well have induced more disruption than co-ordination (112:*197–8*). It also beggars belief that richer peasants would have acceded to the higher rates of taxation wanted for faster industrial capital accumulation or that the middling mass of the peasantry would have easily been persuaded to join collective farms.

Yet other party officials at the centre and in the localities, despite rejecting the Opposition's case, felt the same urge to accelerate the drive towards economic modernisation and military security. Stalin was one of them. Their inclination was reinforced by each successive crisis, at home or abroad, that had to be endured. The NEP had few unembarrassed apologists like Bukharin. Already in the tax year 1925–6 the ascendant party leadership was finding the itch to unsettle its own policy irresistible. A fiscal law was introduced discriminating heavily against the richer peasants in order to raise additional revenues for investment in state industrial enterprises. Bukharin was overruled. The result in 1927 was a lower level of grain marketings. Simultaneously Gosplan, the state central planning agency, was under orders to draft a Five-Year Plan for quicker industrialisation. The food supplies crisis brought Stalin in January 1928 to visit the Urals and western Siberia to requisition grain by main force. Financial experts forecasting chaos from the First Five-Year Plan were silenced; and a show trial of engineers in Shakhty kept the remaining doubters in management quiet. Inside the party, Bukharin's suggestions came to be excoriated as a Right Deviation from Bolshevism. Targets for industrial growth were raised steeply. In order to secure food supplies and also to boost grain exports (which would facilitate the purchase of foreign technology) it was determined to push peasants forcibly into collective farms, and, lest resistance be shown, the minority of kulaks were refused permission to stay on their land. Hundreds of thousands were shipped to Siberia. The terrorised peasantry, starving in the countryside by 1932, migrated in their millions to the towns in search of work and food.

78

The lunges into forced-rate industrialisation and forcible mass collectivisation bring us to the boundaries of this account. At the end of the 1920s a transformation was put in motion which equalled the Revolution of 1917 in importance. Stalin had only the most sketchy programme at the outset of the first Five-Year Plan. Initially he and his associates apparently assumed that they would be able both to raise the workers' material standard of living and provide most collective farms with tractors by 1933. Of such colossal miscalculations was the scheme to terminate the NEP composed.

Stalin undertook an act of will. In a century that has produced not only him but also Hitler and Churchill, who would deny that individual politicians can make an egregious impact upon their times? Lenin, too, was a political giant. A plethora of decisions would never have been taken, or at least would have been formulated with substantial differences, if he had not existed. Nonetheless neither Lenin nor Stalin could operate without organised backing. The ending of the NEP, in particular, was a perennial possibility throughout its time-span. The desire for a more closely administered society and economy was not peculiar to full-time party officials. Similar feelings were expressed inside the party's youth organisation and in the political police. In the educational establishment, voices were raised for radically new policies. Several literary groups spoke likewise. At the same time, in the factories, there were murmurings of discontent that wages and conditions remained poor. The case is sometimes put that Stalin merely responded to these pressures. This is unconvincing. Rather it was that Stalin and his associates in the central party leadership utilised the pressures and deliberately amplified them. Disenchantment with the NEP was not universal; and, where it existed, it was inchoate: there was little consideration of what should replace it. Stalin's group gave the break its shape. And, as the enormous expansion of industry and education and administration gathered pace, so social mobility increased. Greater numbers of people had an interest in the maintenance of the new system. Promotions were frequent. Thus the massive violence which accompanied the remoulding of the Soviet state and its economy did not preclude the wide cultivation of areas of social support. 1927 therefore was an historic landmark. It divides the unstable edifice of the early post-revolutionary period from the years when an imposingly firm structure of state and society was erected in the USSR. In important respects, it lasts to this day.

Afterword

The Revolution of 1917 was a culmination and a beginning; an old order was ended, a new order inaugurated. But the events were also an interruption. Economic achievement had been substantial before the First World War; it was corroborated under the NEP. The social transformation initiated in the late imperial era was resumed in the early 1920s. Both Nikolai II's government and the Bolsheviks facilitated such modernisation: state economic intervention was not negligible before 1917; it was massive thereafter. But the drive towards modernity was not generated only by political action from on high. Society sustained its own thrust towards change. By 1914, the tsarist authorities could no longer subject the population to close and comprehensive control. Only spasmodic repression was practicable. The Bolshevik party amassed greater resources for coercion; but it, too, met with resistance from sections of the working class and the peasantry in the civil war. Concessions were inevitable by 1921. There were other continuities between the two regimes. Free political competition was absent in both. Abject poverty persisted widely. Ideological intolerance spanned the years before and after 1917. And, above all, the country's basic requirements were unchanged. In the first decade of Bolshevik rule it remained as urgent to increase economic strength and military capacity as in the reigns of the last two emperors, and the vigour of the pursuit of material progress, while producing positive results, also accentuated points of weakness. Social tensions remained. Recurrent crises attended the national economy; agriculture in particular was susceptible to periodic, crushing failure.

The imperial regime's instabilities were exposed in 1905 and 1914, and the monarchy collapsed in February 1917. The

81

Great War had induced the final, crippling strain. But what little agreement had united the foes of tsarism quickly disappeared. The months after February saw workers, soldiers and peasants unready to accept most forms of authority associated with the older order. Their demands were initially ratified by the October seizure of power. Some gains were permanent. The entrance of workers into administrative posts commenced (and this was not simply a phenomenon of the Five-Year Plans). Working-class cultural pride was fostered. Property rights were drastically altered, and labour relations, except in the civil war, were more relaxed. Peasants benefited from the removal of landlordism. Perhaps, too, technical personnel were not entirely displeased with the contrast between Lenin's and Nikolai II's government. In any case, the Bolsheviks in government were much more effective in manipulating their way towards obtaining acceptance of their monopoly of state authority.

Yet the chances of the Revolution's evolution down a peaceful, gradualist line were never great. 1917 unchained a host of contradictory and, all too often, unrealistic goals. Worse still, there was a precipitous decline into economic catastrophe between 1917 and 1920. Scarcity nurtured struggle. In addition, the country's cultural and social traditions restricted the general willingness, after the brief tranquillity of spring 1917, to settle political disputes amicably; and the Bolsheviks, having been brought into existence in such a society, added to the dimensions of political ruthlessness. The civil war had enduring, brutalising consequences. And several crucial practical and theoretical restraints upon the scope of state power had been brusquely removed in Lenin's lifetime. There was no unavoidable passage towards Stalinism by the end of the 1920s. But it was always a possibility. The magnitude of the rupture with the NEP will never be underestimated. The early Five-Year Plans catapulted the USSR in the direction of full industrial and technical modernisation at last; and the potentiality for the defeat of a mighty aggressor such as Nazi Germany came within range (although it is still a moot point whether the continuance of the NEP would necessarily have left the Soviet Union militarily helpless in 1941). But these successes must not dazzle our judgement.

Forced-rate industrialisation and forcible collectivisation caused horrendous and unjustifiable social torment. Stalin, moreover, claimed too much material improvement through his policies. He ignored the progress already made in the late imperial and early Soviet epochs; industrialisation was in motion before his political ascendancy commenced. And the difficulties faced by those in the USSR seeking to introduce initiative and technological sophistication to the present-day Soviet economy ought to dissuade other countries from wanting to take the Stalinist road to industrialisation.

Select Bibliography

[1] A. M. Anfimov, *Krupnoe pomeshchich'e khozyaistvo Evropeiskoi Rossii. (Konets XIX – nachalo XX veka)* (Moscow, 1969).

[2] A. M. Anfimov and I. F. Makarov, 'Novye dannye o zemlevladenii Evropeiskoi Rossii', *Istoriya SSSR* (1974), no.1.

[3] D. Atkinson, *The End Of The Russian Land Commune, 1905–1930* (Stanford, 1983).

[4] A. Ya. Avrekh, *Tsarizm i IV-aya Duma, 1912–1914 gg.* (Moscow, 1981).

[5] P. Bairoch, 'Niveaux de développement économique de 1800 à 1910', *Annales* (November–December 1965).

[6] A. Bennigsen and M. Broxup, *The Islamic Threat to the Soviet State* (London, 1983).

[7] F. Benvenuti, *I Bolscevichi e L'Armata Rossa, 1918–1922* (Naples, 1983).

[8] V. Bonnell, *The Roots of Rebellion: Workers' Politics and Organisations in St Petersburg and Moscow, 1900–1914* (Berkeley, 1983).

[9] V. Brovkin, 'The Mensheviks' Political Come-back: The Elections to the Provincial City Soviets in Spring 1918', *Russian Review* (1983), no. 1.

[10] E. H. Carr and R. W. Davies, *Foundations of a Planned Economy, 1926–1929*, vol. 1 (London, 1969).

[11] J. Channon, 'The Bolsheviks, Land Reform and the Peasantry', unpublished Essex conference paper, May 1984.

[12] S. F. Cohen, *Bukharin and the Bolshevik Revolution. A Political Biography, 1888–1938* (London, 1974).

[13] O. Crisp, 'Labour and Industrialisation in Russia', *Cambridge Economic History of Europe*, vol. 7, part 2 (Cambridge, 1978).

[14] O. Crisp, *Studies in the Russian Economy before 1914* (London, 1976).

[15] V. P. Danilov, *Sovetskaya dokolkhoznaya derevnya: naselenie, zemlepol'zovanie, khozyaistvo* (Moscow, 1977).

[16] V. P. Danilov, 'Sovetskaya nalogovaya politika v dokolkhoznoi derevne', in I. M. Volkov (ed.), *Oktyabr' i sovetskoe krest'yanstvo, 1917–1927 gg.* (Moscow, 1977).

[17] R. W. Davies, *The Development of the Soviet Budgetary System* (Cambridge, 1958).

[18] R. W. Davies, *The Socialist Offensive: The Collectivisation of Soviet Agriculture, 1929–1930* (London, 1980).

[19] R. W. Davies, 'Trotskij and the Debate on Industrialisation in the USSR', in F. Gori (ed.), *Pensiero e Azione Politica di Lev Trockij* (Florence, 1983), vol. 1.

[20] M. Dewar, *Labour Policy in the USSR, 1917–1928* (London, 1956).

[21] V. Z. Drobizhev, *Glavnyi shtab sotsialisticheskoi promyshlennosti* (Moscow, 1966).

[22] V. Z. Drobizhev, A. K. Sokolov and V. A. Ustinov, *Rabochii klass Sovetskoi Rossii v pervyi god proletarskoi diktatury* (Moscow, 1975).

[23] S. M. Dubrovskii, *Sel'skoe khozyaistvo i krest'yanstvo Rossii v period imperializma* (Moscow, 1975).

[24] S. M. Dubrovskii, *Stolypinskaya zemel'naya reforma, Iz istorii sel'skogo khozyaistva i krest'yanstva Rossii v nachale XX veka* (Moscow, 1963).

[25] C. Duval, 'Yakov M. Sverdlov and the All-Russian Central Executive Committee of Soviets (VTsIK): A Study in Bolshevik Consolidation of Power, October 1917–July 1918', *Soviet Studies* (1979), no. 1.

[26] V. S. Dyakin *et al.*, *Krizis samoderzhaviya v Rossii, 1895–1917* (Leningrad, 1984).

[27] V. S. Dyakin, *Russkaya burzhuaziya i tsarizm v gody pervoi mirovoi voiny, 1914–1917* (Leningrad, 1967).

[28] R. C. Elwood, *Russian Social-Democracy In The Underground. A Study of the RSDRP in the Ukraine, 1907–1914* (Assen, 1974).

[29] T. Emmons, 'The Zemstvo in Historical Perspective', in T. Emmons (ed.), *The Zemstvo in Russia: An Experiment in Local Self-Government* (Cambridge, 1982).

[30] M. E. Falkus, *The Industrialisation of Russia, 1700–1914* (London, 1972).

[31] M. Ferro, 'The Aspirations of Russian Society', in R. Pipes (ed.), *Revolutionary Russia* (Harvard, 1968).

[32] S. Fitzpatrick, 'Ordzhonikidze's Takeover of Vesenkha: A Case Study in Soviet Bureaucratic Politics', *Soviet Studies* (1985), no. 2.

[33] S. Fitzpatrick, 'Sex and Revolution: An Examination of Literacy and Statistical Data on the Mores of Soviet Students in the 1920s', *Journal of Modern History* (June 1978).

[34] L. S. Gaponenko, *Rabochii klass Rossii v 1917 godu* (Moscow, 1970).

[35] P. W. Gatrell, 'Industrial Expansion in Tsarist Russia, 1908–1914', *Economic History Review* (1982), no. 1.

[36] A. Gerschenkron, 'Agrarian Policies and Industrialisation: Russia, 1861–1917', *Cambridge Economic History of Europe*, vol. 6, part 2 (Cambridge, 1966).

[37] A. Gerschenkron, 'The Rate of Growth of Industrial Production in Russia Since 1885', *Journal of Economic History* (1947), no. 7–S.

[38] I. Getzler, *Kronstadt, 1917–1921. The Fate of a Soviet Democracy* (Cambridge, 1983).

[39] G. Gill, *Peasants and Government in the Russian Revolution* (London, 1979).

[40] E. V. Gimpel'son, *Velikii Oktyabr' i stanovlenie sovetskoi sistemy upravleniya narodnym khozyaistvom (noyabr' 1917–1920 gg.)* (Moscow, 1977).

[41] E. V. Gimpel'son, *'Voennyi kommunizm': politika, praktika, ideologiya* (Moscow, 1973).

[42] I. A. Gladkov, *Sovetskoe narodnoe khozyaistvo v 1921–1925 gg.* (Moscow, 1960).

[43] R. Glickman, 'The Russian Factory Woman, 1880–1914', in D. Atkinson, A. Dallin and G. Warshofsky Lapidus (eds), *Women In Russia* (Stanford, 1977).

[44] P. Gregory, 'Economic Growth and Structural Change in Tsarist Russia: A Case of Modern Economic Growth?', *Soviet Studies* (December 1967).

[45] P. Gregory, *Russian National Income, 1885–1913* (Cambridge, 1982).

[46] L. H. Haimson, 'The Problem of Urban Stability in Russia, 1905–1917', *Slavic Review* (1964), no. 5 and (1965), no. 1.

[47] G. M. Hamburg, *Politics of the Russian Nobility, 1881–1905* (New Brunswick, 1984).

[48] M. Hildermeier, *Die Sozialrevolutionäre Partei Russlands. Agrarsozialismus und Modernisierung im Zarenreich (1900–1914)* (Cologne–Vienna, 1976).

[49] H. Hogan, 'The Reorganisation of Work Processes in the St Petersburg Metal-working Industry, 1901–14', *Russian Review* (1983), no. 2.

[50] G. A. Hosking, *The Russian Constitutional Experiment: Government and Duma, 1907–1914* (Cambridge, 1973).

[51] R. E. Johnson, *Peasant and Proletarian. The Working Class of Moscow in the Late Nineteenth Century* (Leicester, 1979).

[52] A. Kahan, 'Capital Formation During the Period of Early Industrialisation in Russia, 1890–1913', *Cambridge Economic History of Europe*, vol. 7, part 2 (Cambridge, 1978).

[53] E. M. Kayden and A. N. Antsiferov, *The Co-operative Movement In Russia During The War* (New Haven, 1929).

[54] J. L. H. Keep, *The Russian Revolution: A Study In Mass Mobilisation* (London, 1976).

[55] P. Kenez, 'A Profile of the Pre-Revolutionary Officer Corps', *California Slavic Studies* (1973), no. 7.

[56] T. Khitanina, *Khlebnaya torgovlya Rossii, 1875–1914 gg. (Ocherki pravitel'stvennoi politiki)* (Leningrad, 1978)

[57] P. A. Khromov, *Ekonomicheskoe razvitie Rossii. Ocherki ekonomiki Rossii s drevneishikh vremen do Velikoi Oktyabr'skoi revolyutsii* (Moscow, 1967).

[58] A. Khryashcheva, *Krest'yanstvo v voine i revolyutsii* (Moscow, 1921).

[59] Yu. I. Kir'yanov, *Zhiznennyi uroven' rabochikh Rossii (konets XIX – nachalo XX vv.)* (Moscow, 1979).

[60] S. M. Klyatskin, *Na zashchite Oktyabrya. Organizatsiya regulyarnoi armii i militsionnoe stroitel'stvo v Sovetskoi respublike, 1917–1920* (Moscow, 1965).

[61] D. Koenker, *Moscow Workers and the 1917 Revolution* (Princeton, 1981).

[62] D. Kol'tsov, 'Rabochie v 1890–1904 gg.', in L. Martov, P. Maslov and A. Potresov (eds), *Obshchestvennoe dvizhenie v Rossii v nachale XX-go veka*, vol. 1 (St Petersburg, 1909).

[63] A. P. Korelin, *Dvoryanstvo poreformennoi Rossii, 1861–1905 gg.* (Moscow, 1979).

[64] I. D. Koval'chenko, 'Sootnoshenie krest'yanskogo i pomeshchich'ego khozyaistva v zemlevladel'cheskom proizvodstve kapitalisticheskoi Rossii', in L. I. Ivanov *et al.* (eds), *Problemy sotsial'no-ekonomicheskoi istorii Rossii. Sbornik statei* (Moscow, 1971).

[65] N. A. Kravchuk, *Massovoe krest'yanskoe dvizhenie v Rossii nakanune Oktyabrya (mart–oktyabr' 1917 g.). Po materialam velikorosskikh gubernii Evropeiskoi Rossii* (Moscow, 1971).

[66] E. E. Kruze, *Polozhenie rabochego klassa Rossii v 1900–1914 gg.* (Leningrad, 1976).

[67] L. Lande, 'Some Statistics of the Unification Congress, August 1917', in L. H. Haimson (ed.), *The Mensheviks from the Revolution of 1917 to the Second World War* (Chicago, 1974).

[68] V. Ya. Laverychev, *Gosudarstvo i monopolii v dorevolyutsionnoi Rossii* (Moscow, 1982).

[69] G. Leggett, *The Cheka: Lenin's Political Police. The All-Russian Extraordinary Commission for Combating Counter-Revolution and Sabotage (December 1917 to February 1922)* (Oxford, 1981).

[70] D. Lieven, 'The Russian Civil Service under Nicholas II: Some Variations on the Bureaucratic Theme', *Jahrbücher für Geschichte Osteuropas* (1981), no. 29.

[71] U. Liszkowski, *Zwischen Liberalismus und Imperialismus. Die zaristische Aussenpolitik vor dem Ersten Weltkrieg im Urteil Miljukovs und der Kadettenpartei, 1905–1914* (Stuttgart, 1974).

[72] F. Lorimer, *The Population Of the Soviet Union: History And Prospects* (Geneva, 1946).

[73] D. Mandel, *The Petrograd Workers and the Fall of the Old Regime* (London, 1983).

[74] D. Mandel, *The Petrograd Workers and the Soviet Seizure of Power. From the July Days, 1917 to July 1918* (London, 1984).

[75] R. T. Manning, *The Crisis of the Old Order in Russia: Gentry and Government* (Princeton, 1982).

[76] E. Mawdsley, *The Russian Revolution and the Baltic Fleet. War and Politics, February 1917–April 1918* (London, 1978).

[77] S. Merl, *Der Agrarmarkt und die Neue Ökonomische Politik. Die Anfänge staatlicher Lenkung der Landwirtschaft in der Sowjetunion 1925–1928* (Munich–Vienna, 1981).

[78] S. Milligan, 'The Petrograd Bolsheviks and Social Insurance, 1914–1917', *Soviet Studies* (1968–9), no. 3.

[79] I. I. Mints, *Istoriya velikogo Oktyabrya*, vol. 1, *Sverzhenie samoderzhaviya* (Moscow, 1967).

[80] W. Mosse, 'Revolution in Saratov (October–November 1917)', *Slavonic and East European Review* (October 1981).

[81] R. Munting, 'A Note on Gentry Landownership in European Russia', *New Zealand Slavonic Journal* (1978), no. 1.

[82] N. M. Naimark, *Terrorists and Social Democrats. The Russian Revolutionary Movement Under Alexander III* (Harvard, 1983).

[83] O. A. Narkiewicz, *The Making of the Soviet State Apparatus* (Manchester, 1970).

[84] A. S. Nifontov, *Zernovoe proizvodstvo Rossii vo vtoroi polovine XIX veka* (Moscow, 1974).

[85] T. V. Osipova, 'Razvitie sotsialisticheskoi revolyutsii v derevne v pervyi god diktatury proletariata', in I. M. Volkov *et al.* (eds), *Oktyabr' i sovetskoe krest'yanstvo, 1917–1922 gg.* (Moscow, 1977).

[86] J. Pallot, 'Agrarian Modernization on Peasant Farms in the Era of Capitalism', in J. H. Bater and R. A. French (eds), *Studies in Russian Historical Geography*, vol. 2 (London, 1983).

[87] R. Pearson, *The Russian Moderates and the Crisis of Tsarism, 1914–1917* (London, 1977).

[88] M. Perrie, *The Agrarian Policy of the Russian Socialist-Revolutionary Party from its Origins through the Revolution of 1905–1907* (Cambridge, 1976).

[89] R. Pethybridge, *The Social Prelude To Stalinism* (London, 1974).

[90] Yu. A. Polyakov, *Perekhod k nepu i sovetskoe krest'yanstvo* (Moscow, 1967).

[91] M. Pushkin, 'Raznochintsy in the University: Government Policy and Social Change in Nineteenth Century Russia', *International Review of Social History* (1981), part 1.

[92] A. Rabinowitch, *The Bolsheviks Come to Power* (New York, 1976).

[93] O. H. Radkey, *The Agrarian Foes of Communism. Promise and Default of the Russian Socialist-Revolutionaries, February to October 1917* (Cambridge, 1950).

[94] O. H. Radkey, *The Election to the Russian Constituent Assembly of 1917* (Harvard, 1950).

[95] D. J. Raleigh, 'Revolutionary Politics in Provincial Russia: The Tsaritsyn "Republic" in 1917', *Slavic Review* (summer 1981).

[96] A. G. Rashin, 'Dinamika promyshlennykh kadrov SSSR za 1917–1958 gg.', in D. A. Baevskii (ed.), *Izmeneniya v chislennosti i sostave sovetskogo klassa* (Moscow, 1961).

[97] A. G. Rashin, *Formirovanie rabochego klassa Rossii. Istoriko-ekonomicheskie ocherki* (Moscow, 1958).

[98] A. G. Rashin, *Naselenie Rossii za 100 let* (Moscow, 1956).

[99] E. A. Rees, 'Rabkrin and the Soviet System of State Control, 1920–1930', unpublished Ph.D. thesis (University of Birmingham, 1982).

[100] A. J. Rieber, *Merchants and Entrepreneurs in Imperial Russia* (North Carolina, 1982).

[101] T. H. Rigby, *Communist Party Membership in the USSR, 1917–1967* (Princeton, 1968).

[102] T. H. Rigby, 'The First Proletarian Government', *British Journal of Political Science* (January 1974).

[103] T. H. Rigby, *Lenin's Government: Sovnarkom, 1917–1922* (Cambridge, 1979).

[104] J. Riordan, *Sport in Soviet Society. Development of Sport and Physical Education in Russia and the USSR* (Cambridge, 1977).

[105] H. Rogger, *Russia in the Age of Modernisation and Revolution, 1881–1917* (London, 1983).

[106] W. H. Roobol, *Tsereteli – A Democrat in the Russian Revolution. A Political Biography* (The Hague, 1976).

[107] W. G. Rosenberg, *Liberals in the Russian Revolution: The Constitutional Democratic Party, 1917–1921* (Princeton, 1974).

[108] J. Schneiderman, *Sergei Zubatov and Revolutionary Marxism. The Struggle for the Working Class in Tsarist Russia* (Ithaca, 1976).

[109] R. Service, 'From Polyarchy to Hegemony: The Party's Role in the Construction of the Central Institutions of the Soviet State, 1917–1919', *Sbornik* (1984), no. 10.

[110] R. Service, 'Lenin and the October Revolution: The First Two Hundred Days', unpublished Essex conference paper, May 1984.

[111] R. Service, *Lenin: A Political Life*, vol. 1, *The Strengths of Contradiction* (London, 1985).

[112] R. Service, *The Bolshevik Party in Revolution: A Study in Organisational Change, 1917–1923* (London, 1979).

[113] H. Seton-Watson, *The Russian Empire, 1801–1917* (Oxford, 1967).

[114] T. Shanin, *The Awkward Class. Political Sociology of Peasantry in a Developing Society: Russia, 1910–1925* (Oxford, 1972).

[115] J. Y. Simms, 'The Crisis in Russian Agriculture at the End of the Nineteenth Century: A Different View', *Slavic Review* (1977), no. 3.

[116] M. Smith, 'War, Autocracy and Public Men: Grain Procurement and Politics, 1914–1917', unpublished research seminar paper (CREES, Birmingham, n.d.).

[117] S. Smith, *Red Petrograd. Revolution in the Factories, 1917–1918* (Cambridge, 1983).

[118] Yu. B. Solov'ev, *Samoderzhavie i dvoryanstvo v kontse XX-go veka* (Leningrad, 1973).

[119] J. D. Sontag, 'Tsarist Debts and Tsarist Foreign Policy', *Slavic Review* (1968), no. 4.

[120] S. Sternheimer, 'Administration for Development: The Emerging Bureaucratic Elite, 1920–1930', in W. K. Pintner and D. K. Rowney, *Russian Officialdom: the Bureaucratisation of Russian society from the seventeenth to the twentieth century* (London, 1980).

[121] N. Stone, *The Eastern Front, 1914–1917* (London, 1975).

[122] R. G. Suny, *The Baku Commune, 1917–1918. Class and Nationality in the Russian Revolution* (Princeton, 1972).

[123] A. C. Sutton, *Western Technology and Soviet Economic Development, 1917–1930* (Stanford, 1968).

[124] G. Swain, *Russian Social-Democracy and the Legal Labour Movement, 1906–1914* (London, 1983).

[125] T. Swietochowski, *Russian Azerbaijan, 1905–1920. The Shaping of a National Identity in a Muslim Community* (Cambridge, 1985).

[126] Y. Taniuchi, *The Village Gathering in Russia in the mid-1920s* (Birmingham, 1968).

[127] R. Taylor, *The Politics of the Soviet Cinema, 1917–1929* (Cambridge, 1979).

[128] *Tret'ya vserossiiskaya konferentsiya professional'nykh soyuzov, 3–11 iyulya (20 29 iyunya st. st.) 1917 goda. Stenograficheskii otchet* (ed. D. Koenker: New York–London, 1982).

[129] P. V. Volobuev, *Ekonomicheskaya politika Vremennogo pravitel'stva* (Moscow, 1962).

[130] *Vos'maya konferentsiya konferentsiya RKP(b), dekabr' 1919 goda. Protokoly* (Moscow, 1961).

[131] R. A. Wade, 'The Rajonnye Sovety of Petrograd: The Role of Local Political Bodies in the Russian Revolution', *Jahrbücher für Geschichte Osteuropas* (1972), no. 2.

[132] R. A. Wade, *The Russian Search for Peace, February–October 1917* (Stanford, 1967).

[133] S. G. Wheatcroft, 'Famine and Epidemic Crises in Russia, 1918–

1922: The Case of Saratov', *Annales de Démographie Historique* (1983).

[134] S. G. Wheatcroft, 'Grain Production and Utilisation in Russia and the USSR before Collectivisation', unpublished Ph.D. thesis (University of Birmingham, 1980).

[135] S. G. Wheatcroft, 'The Balance of Grain Production and Utilisation in Russia before and during the Revolution', unpublished research seminar paper (CREES, Birmingham, 1982).

[136] S. G. Wheatcroft, 'The Use of Meteorological Data to Supplement and Analyse Data on Grain Yields in Russia and the USSR, 1883–1950', unpublished research seminar paper (Cambridge, 1982).

[137] S. G. Wheatcroft, R. W. Davies and J. M. Cooper, 'Soviet Industrialisation Reconsidered: Some Preliminary Conclusions About Economic Developments between 1926 and 1941', revised and unpublished research paper (CREES, Birmingham, 1982).

[138] H. J. White, 'The Provisional Government and the Problem of Power in the Provinces, March–October 1917', unpublished Oxford conference paper (January 1982).

[139] A. Wildman, *The End of the Russian Imperial Army: The Old Army and the Soldiers' Revolt (March–April 1917)* (Princeton, 1980).

[140] A. Wood, 'Siberian Exile in Tsarist Russia', *History Today* (September 1980).

[141] I. A. Yurkov, *Ekonomicheskaya politika partii v derevne, 1917–1920* (Moscow, 1980).

[142] P. A. Zaionchkovskii, *Krizis samoderzhaviya na rubezhe 1870–1880 gg.* (Moscow, 1964).

[143] E. Zaleski, *Planning for Economic Growth in the Soviet Union, 1918–1932* (Chapel Hill, 1971).

Map 1

91

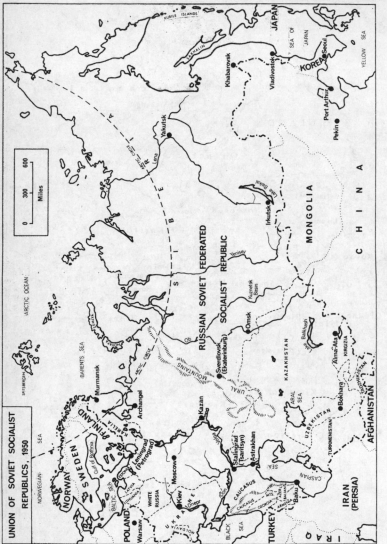

UNION OF SOVIET SOCIALIST
REPUBLICS, 1950

Map 2

Index

Black Sea fleet, 15
'Bloody Sunday', 15
Bolsheviks: 23, 33, 38, 40, 43–5, 47–9,
   50–61, 62–3, 65, 68, 71, 73–6, 77;
   expectations, 23, 43–5, 48, 51, 52;
   central party bodies, 44, 47, 48, 50, 58,
   61–2, 74, 79; local committees, 40, 44,
   58, 66, 74, 79; activists, 40, 44–5, 52;
   rank-and-filers, 44, 67, 76;
   organisational methods, 44–5, 61–2,
   67, 74, 77–8; involvement with
   workers, 23, 40, 45, 55, 75 and with
   peasants, 40, 58, 71–2, 76; *see also*
   Central Committee, Politburo,
   Orgburo, Secretariat and individual
   leaders.
Bolshevism, 23, 43–5, 48, 57, 58, 62, 64,
   66, 75, 79; *see also under* Bolsheviks
Bosnia, 24
Brazil, 3
Brest-Litovsk, treaty of, 54, 60, 61
Britain, 2, 18, 22, 46–7, 64, 68, 70, 77
Brusilov, A.A., 37
Bukharin, N.I., 54, 77, 78
Bulgaria, 6

capital, transfer of political (1918), 60
capital goods: in industry, 7, 22, 26–7,
   69–70, 77; in agriculture, 8, 10, 11, 69,
   77
capitalism in the Russian empire and the
   USSR, 6–8, 14, 38–9, 54, 68; *see also*
   agrarian capitalism, industrial
   capitalism; *and under* agriculture and
   industry
Caspian Sea, 3, 42
Catherine II, 4
Caucasus, 5
censorship, 3, 18, 71
central Asia, 2, 30, 73
Central Committee (Bolshevik), 44, 45,
   47–8, 53, 58, 61–2, 75
Central Control Commission
   (Bolshevik), 75
centralisation of state power: under
   absolute monarchy, 1, 3–4, 16–17, 18,
   30; under the Bolsheviks, 58–60, 61–2,
   74, 79
Central Powers, 28, 54; *see also*
   Austria–Hungary, Germany
central Russia, 21, 27, 51, 57, 59
Chaplin, C., 71
Cheka, 59, 62, 65, 73

chemical industry, 7
Chernov, V.M., 36–7, 42, 47, 57
Chile, 66
China, 2, 60
Christian belief, 72; *see also* Church,
   priests
Church, Russian Orthodox, 5, 17, 18,
   32–3, 51, 73; *see also* Christian belief,
   priests
Churchill, W., 79
cinema, 71
civil servants: under absolute
   monarchy, 5, 10, 13, 70; under
   Provisional Government, 33, 34; under
   Soviet government, 56, 60, 62, 70, 73,
   75, 76
Civil War, 59, 60–7
climate, 2, 7, 21
closures of factories, *see under* factories
coal, 3, 7, 38, 75
coalition: in the Provisional
   Government, 36–7, 41, 44, 47, 57; in
   Sovnarkom, 58, 59, 61
collective farms, 58, 77, 78, 79
collectivisation, mass, 78
committees of public safety, 32
committees of the village poor, 63, 65
communes, land, 9, 13, 14, 15, 20–1, 40,
   56–7, 72
communications, 3, 64
communism, *see* Bolshevism,
   anti-Bolshevik communism
Communist International, 62
Congress of Soviets: First, 41; Second,
   48, 49, 51
conscription, 28, 29, 62, 67
conservatives, 16, 24, 30; *see also*
   Octobrists
Constituent Assembly, 31, 32, 59, 61
constitution, demands for, 15, 31
Constitutional Democrats, *see* Kadets
consumer goods: from industry, 7, 27,
   53, 68; from agriculture, *see under*
   agriculture
continuity between pre-1917 and
   post-1917 epochs: economy, 53–4, 57,
   68, 69, 71, 77, 81–2; politics, 59, 73,
   75–6, 81–2; society, 57, 70, 71, 72, 73,
   81–2
co-operatives, 20
corruption, 5, 17, 22, 53, 75
Cossacks, 51, 64
cotton, 8

94

99

55, 56, 59; personnel, 51, 58, 59, 74;
  internal organisation, 51, 58–9, 62
sown area, *see under* landed nobility,
  peasants
Spain, 2
Spartakists, 66
sport, 76
Stalin, I.V., 19, 64, 74, 77, 78, 79, 83
standard of living, material: under
  absolute monarchy, 10, 11–13, 15,
  22–3, 28–9; under Provisional
  Government, 33, 38, 39; under Soviet
  government, 53, 54–5, 57, 63, 66, 71–2
State Conference, 47
State Council, 17
state monopoly of trade in grain, 27, 38,
  57, 63
state ownership in industry: under
  absolute monarchy, 6; under Soviet
  government, 51, 53, 55–6, 63, 68
steel, 7, 77
steppes, 2
Stockholm Conference, 37
Stolypin, P.A., 16, 17, 21
Straits of Dardanelles, 2, 25
street demonstrations, 15, 23, 31, 36, 59,
  76
strikes, 12, 23, 25, 29, 30–1, 38, 67, 70
students, 13
sugar beet, 8
Sundary schools, 20
Supreme Council of the National
  Economy, 75
surveyors, 72
Sverdlov, Y.M., 52
Switzerland, 44

Tambov, 67
Tannenberg, battle of, 25
tariffs, 6, 11
taxation: 1; direct taxes, 1, 68, 78;
  indirect taxes, 6
technical sophistication, *see under*
  agriculture, industry
terror: 'individual', 14; mass (Red and
  White), 59, 65, 73
Texas, 7
textile industry, 7
timber, 3
Tolstoi, L.N., 18
tractors, 77, 79
trade unions: under absolute monarchy,
  12, 14, 15, 20; under Provisional

Government, 40; under Soviet
  government, 56, 71, 76
Transcaucasus, 2, 19, 52
transport, 3, 38, 53, 64
Trotski, L.D., 23, 40, 46, 48, 49, 54, 58,
  62, 64, 65, 70, 77
Tsaritsyn, 42, 46
Tsereteli, I.G., 36, 40, 41, 47
Turkestan, 8
Turkey, 19; *see also* Ottoman empire

Ukraine, 2, 8, 10, 21, 27, 32, 37, 46,
  54–5, 57, 60, 63, 65, 67; *see also Rada*,
  Ukranian Soviet Republic
Ukrainians, 3, 19, 52
Ukrainian Soviet Republic, 74
'under-government' in Russia, 18–19,
  75
underground, political, 14
unemployment, 23, 38, 56, 60, 77
Union of the Russian People, 24
Union of Soviet Socialist Republics, *see*
  USSR
United Opposition (Bolshevik), 77
universities, 13
Urals, 8, 60, 75
USA, 2, 3, 22, 46–7
USSR, ix, 19, 74, 77, 82, 83
utopianism, 56, 82

Versailles, treaty of, 70
violence in society, 15, 33–4, 40, 55, 57,
  67; *see also* civil war, dictatorship, terror
Vistula, battle of, 67
Vladivostock, 3
vodka, 20
Volga region, 7, 52, 53, 60, 61, 68
Volga, river, 63
Volunteer Army, 59, 61; *see also* White
  armies *under* army

wages, *see under* workers
'War Commission', 64; *see also* Civil War
War-Industry Committees, 30
Warsaw, 15, 66
wheat production, 7, 20–1, 27, 53, 66, 69
White armies, *see under* army
Winter Palace, 48
Witte, S.Y., 4, 17
women in revolution, 15, 31, 71
woodland, 13, 15
workers: 1, 9, 14, 25, 65, 66, 71, 73, 82;
  wages, 12, 28, 33, 38, 71; living

conditions, 11, 22, 28–9, 38, 56, 60, 66, 71, 79; training, 9, 12; aspirations, 14, 33, 38–9, 42, 58, 67, 76; skilled workers, 12, 28, 39, 66; unskilled workers, 12, 39; number of workers, 9, 28, 38, 71; discontent, 12, 14, 15, 20, 23, 29, 33, 38, 55, 56, 58, 67, 70–1, 76; revolt and direct social action, 15, 23, 31, 36, 39, 48, 51, 53, 55, 59, 76
Workers' and Peasants' Inspectorate, 75
Workers' and Peasants' Red Army, *see under* army

workers' control, 39, 48, 51, 53, 55
Workers' Opposition (Bolshevik), 68
working class, *see* workers
Wrangel, P.N., 63

Yudenich, N.N., 63

zemlyachestva, 20
zemstva, 9, 14, 16, 17, 30, 32
Zinoviev, G.E., 46, 53, 77